Eclectic Verse

mommy i hear those whispers . . . (again)

William S. Peters, Sr.

inner child press, ltd.

Credits

Author

William S. Peters, Sr.

Editor

hülya n. yılmaz, Ph.D.

Introduction

hülya n. yılmaz, Ph.D.

Commentary

Fahredin B. Shehu

Cover Graphics & Design

William S. Peters Sr.
inner child press, ltd.

General Information

Eclectic Verse
William S. Peters, Sr.

1st Edition: 2019

This Publishing is protected under the Copyright Law as a "Collection". All rights for all submissions are retained by the individual author and or artist. No part of this publishing may be reproduced, transferred in any manner without the prior **WRITTEN CONSENT** of the "Material Owner" or its representative, Inner Child Press International. Any such violation infringes upon the Creative and Intellectual Property of the Owner pursuant to International and Federal Copyright Law. Any queries pertaining to this "Collection" should be addressed to the Publisher of Record.

Publisher Information
Inner Child Press International
www.innerchildpress.com

This Collection is protected under U.S. and International Copyright Laws.

Copyright © 2019: William S. Peters, Sr.

ISBN-13: 978-1-970020-73-1 (inner child press, ltd.)

$ 24.95

My Eclectic Dedication

In loving memory of
Virisa Anne Cohen-Peters
4 July, 1957 – 2 July, 2006

Every Saturday

my Son and i awakened that Saturday morning
the Sun was bright
it was a lovely Spring day

we brushed our teeth
washed our face
as we prepared for our weekly visit
to the market,
needless to say, he was so excited,
we both were

we dressed
in a sort of reverent appreciation
for life,
a warm silence
permeated the air
and we could hear our own hearts beating
with anticipation

we exited the house
that morning about 10 o'clock,
the birds were singing
while digging in the lush green lawns
looking for brunch i guess,
just as they did every Saturday morning
when we went about our quest
to the market

yes, my Son and i were on a mission,
we had things to do
brown bags to fill
with edible discoveries of the day

we jumped in the car
i turned the key
which cranked the engine
and my Son,
he asked if he could drive
i smiled as i did every other Saturday
and i replied
"One Day Soon Son"
he looked at me with a twinkle in his eye
and he said
"OK Daddy . . . Cool"
i chuckled
as we buckled our seatbelts

we pulled out of the driveway,
many of our neighbors were busy
mowing their lawns
tending their flower gardens
and all sorts of Saturday morning things

and this Saturday morning,
just like every Saturday morning
he, my Son waved
and said hello to them all
and told everyone
"we are on the way to the mall"
i softly looked at him in love
and i accepted his perspective in silence
as i do every Saturday

we arrived at the market
and he anxiously bounced in car
in the seat
while i parked it,
when we came to a stop
he hurriedly unbuckled his belt
and i chuckled for i felt
his glee
all in me

he quickly ran to the market
ahead of me . . .
you see,
he had a routine
which was a part of his joy,
his life,
his need,
and before i could plead with him to slow down
he was through the doors
and into the store
seeking to satisfy his heart's wishes

and as i approached
he came back out again
with a smile that had no end
and he exclaimed
"I know what i am going to buy Mommy"
i smiled warmly
and before i could evoke the question "what?"
he spoke of such things in the bakery
like the pastry with nuts
and such
but today he wanted to get Cheesecake
yes Cheesecake
just as he does every Saturday

we both knew that was her favorite,
if she was here with us
she would savor it,
and her favorite of course
was Strawberry

we went into the market
to the bakery
as we did every Saturday,
and John the Baker
came to the counter
and said cheerily
with deliberate flattery
"How can i help you young man?"
and my son beamed in bright wonder
for John had acknowledged him
as a growing equal,
a man soon-to-be . . .

one who could make valid decisions
for himself . . . and his Mother

he placed his order
and John lovingly wrapped it
with a certain and knowing care . . .
he put a special bow of string on it
as he did every Saturday morning

my son surveyed the package
took his order gingerly
and held it
in the crest of his arms
for he did not want his gift damaged,
it was heartfully special to him

we completed our errands in the market,
and we went to the car where we parked it
we got in our seats
our mission complete
we buckled our seatbelts
and we drove home

there was a hanging silence in the car at this time
as we both knew what was to come,
we pulled into the driveway
exited the car
and entered the house
with a prevalent awareness
of each and every now laborious step
we entered the kitchen

my Son unwrapped the Cheesecake
and placed it on the plate,
his Mother's favorite plate,
that which she loved
as long as we could remember

we sat at the table
and we bowed our heads
and offered a prayer
to Mommy
for Mommy was not here,
She was in the world of Spirit

and the prayer we prayed
was that She could hear it

we prayed that Cancer
would never take another Mommy from a child,
and though Mommy has been gone from us a while
we still felt her presence

our tears flowed from within us
and began to drip on the table,
and in a knowing silence
that Mommy was not dead

we each grabbed a napkin
and wiped our eyes
and as we did each and every Saturday
we realized
just how much she still means to us

we gave thanks

and my Son,
the coming Man
did understand
something quite profound
that grounded him,
and that was
that through it all
we must continue to answer the call
every Saturday
every Day
for Mommy
for God
for Us
for
Love Prevails . . .
every Day
every Saturday

x

Table of Contents

My Eclectic Dedication	v
Preface . . . a Humanitarian Story	xvii
Introduction	xxi
Foreword	xxv

The Poetry   1

Wonder . . . Conformity?	3
A Dimension Apart	5
12 Years a Slave	8
1 up . . . Can You Hear the Music?	9
A Poem for Mary	11
Cinderella	13
. . . That We May Live	15
I Am	17
No One	18
A Saba' Queen	20
Which One Do You Feed?	23
Musing	28
A Visit with My Muse	29
The Proof	32
Culpritiousness	33
Poetic Perspectives in Vanity	34
Holy	36

Table of Contents... *continued*

Agendas	38
Listen!	40
Conditions	42
Medusa at the Gate	44
But a Few Billion	45
The Aksum School	48
Damaged	50
and . . . i realize!	51
See . . .	53
Independence Day	54
And Shine . . .	56
With Ribboned Bows	58
Beyond the Room	60
Some Day	61
Catalyst	63
Things	64
Heaven	68
Expansion	69
Neque Fiduciam	73
Critique	74
Inner Conflict	77
what may come	79
The Anatomy of a Poem	80
Horizon	84
Damn, I Am Awakening!	86

Table of Contents ... *continued*

I Affirmed	88
A Poem for the Dead	89
My Horror	91
Dance Music	93
Nez Perce	94
In the Room	96
Fire	97
No!	98
Dysfunction	99
Mantra	101
her story	102
The Internet	107
Black Hole	109
Silently Dying	110
Everybody Hurts	111
Pre-Historic	113
. . . are mine to find	115
I Always Dreamed of . . . You	120
yes, i dream	121
Forever	123
He Had Been Stripped	124
She Walked Leisurely	125
Just Like You	126
Bliss Knew My Name	127
meop drawkcab eht	129

Table of Contents . . . *continued*

Thorns and Storms	130
I Will Not Be Chained	132
Forward Reflections	134
Oceania	135
home . . . come	136
erat scriptum	140
The Life of Death	141
Here I Am	142
Singularity	143
I Am Grateful	144
What Percentage of Human Are You?	145
Muse	146
Sumerian	147
How Could I Forget Her?	148
Breathe	150
Who We Are	152
In the Midst	154
The Sun Always Rises	155
Bengali	156
I Wonder	158
Swimming in the Mud	159
A Prevailing Mindset	160
Our First Time	161
Divinely Flawed	162
Paleo	165

Table of Contents . . . *continued*

Conditional Love	167
I Wish	168
Questions to Ponder . . . or at Least, to Wonder About	170
Discovery	171
The Letter	173
Humanity	175
Smiles	176
A Tribute to Love	177
My Truth	179
Such a Place Exists	181
When I Die	183
I Want to Be	184
The Blood	186
Fire ~ Pyro	189
Melancholy	190
She ~ Her	192
Going Forward . . .	196
The Gift	197
My Love	198
We All Win When . . .	199
the grand charade	200
Indigenous	201
Thus So . . .	202
Lost	204
Observing	206

Table of Contents... *continued*

To Be	207
To Do	209
To Listen	210
NOW	212
She	213
Remembering Mommy	214
The Maori	217
Past Times	218
Of All Things	220
As Zion Comes Home . . . to Me!	222
Same	228
Perniciousness	229
Shine On!	230
Of Dreams . . .	232
The End Game	234
Today and Every Day	236
Eclectic Verse	237

Epilogue 241

about William S. Peters, Sr.	243
a few words from Fahredin B. Shehu . . .	247
A Selection of the Author's Other Books	249

Preface ... a Humanitarian Story

Yesterday, I had the occasion to visit the City of Philadelphia. Upon getting off the train, I exited the station and, being hungry, I went to the hot dog cart and purchased a hot dog with sauerkraut and mustard and an apple juice. Walking down Market Street (the main drag), I noticed a homeless lady sitting in front of one of the department stores with a cup in her hand and a small sign, making her plea to humanity. I, in my "Humanity" or the absence thereof, did notice her, but I insulated myself from feeling any empathy. Well ... about 10 to 20 paces down the sidewalk, I reached in my pocket and pulled out a coined dollar, did a 180 degree about face and deposited it in her cup. She softly replied: "Thank You". I mumbled, "you are welcome". I was embarrassed to even face myself and the Universe. 1 Dollar ... just 1 Dollar allowed me to be blessed. As I was walking away, I realized how much I had been blessed to come to this realization of self. We can make a difference ... even if it is a small one!

Many of us saunter through our life paths dumbed down, callous and indifferent to the world and its condition around us ... daily. We hear the voices within us, albeit the Voice of Empathy, Compassion or Love for our world and our Brothers and Sisters who co-inhabit it with us, and we somehow manage to silent those voices, thereby doing damage to our selves and thus, retard our own awakening. This one incident for me reaffirmed how far I still yet have to go, for I too am susceptible to those errant voices of reasonable darkness that isolate me from the potential beauties of self and the world around me, found in that simple word given to me as a gift from this lady sitting in front of a department store in the City of Philadelphia. She simply said, "Thank You" ... what a wonderful gift!

yes, he was homeless

he sat on the sidewalk
near the corner
by a bus stop
where the passengers would pass him by

he was stuck in a convoluted vortex
between despair and hope,
not necessarily of his own doing

he was just looking for a way to cope
with the invisible rope
around the neck of his dead dreams

yes, he was homeless

it has been quite some time,
more than he could even remember
since he saw his little girl
yes, she and his family were his world,
but she probably was not little anymore
it has been so many years,
so many tears,
and all the fears
he once embraced
have now fled,
for all that he once prized
has been bled
from his prideful grasp
right before his eyes . . .
his family,
his home
and now, he has been destined to roam
these streets of continuing anguish

yes, he was homeless

as he spent his days
in his own chosen ways,
he has never held out his hand
to beg

though his life was out of hand,
there still resided an uncertain pride
and dignity . . .
his humanity,
with a somewhat suspect certainty

yes, he was homeless

in spite of himself,
he tried
and would not allow his noble spirit
to be denied
yes, he defied
the indifference to his suffering
and perhaps, the societal expectations
that told him to give up on life
to just become a part of the collection of statistics
and rollover and die,
but still he vied
for more

yes, he was homeless

somewhere, buried deeply in his heart
there still lived something warm
and it was all his alone
he found this quite special
it was the only thing left
yes, it was his alone
and it could not be taken
nor forsaken

yes, he was homeless

there were pictures there he prized
he held them forever in his inner eye,
embraced them,
saw his face in them
there were pictures of a "White Picket Fence"
with a gate
that somehow, he believed
would alter his fate

as it led to a brighter day,
and this dark night would dissipate,
become sunshine once again
and then he could brightly,
nightly
embrace his joy of expectation one more time

in this same vision,
he saw sidewalks,
but the only apparent purpose they served
was for little red wagons,
Hopscotch, skates,
the endless smiles and sunshine
upon the face of the children
and such,
a place where he could touch,
a place in space not forgotten

and though he was homeless,
he still had a heart
his sanity
and his heart were the home
of his humanity
so, though he was homeless,
he still was so much more
than "the man at the bus stop"

and though he was just the man
on the sidewalk
of our city,
homeless
it is not pity one should give
perhaps a meal, your heart, a gesture, a smile . . .
stop and take some time to converse for a while,
share your humanity,
share your heart,
for therein resides the home
. . . of us all

yes, he was homeless

Introduction

Throughout my academic career that spans over forty years, countless research projects, scholarly papers and treatises, critical essays and book manuscripts – all of literary nature, have come my way. In due process, a thorough familiarity with the field-specific traditions as far as Turkish, German and North American literature became a must. As an avid student of my field, I responded to its demands to the best of my ability as an educator, but also as a self-appointed lifetime learner. The teaching-learning / learning-teaching dynamics I fell in love with during my early post-graduate employment has not left me just because I am now retired from my academic duties. Along the way, I have acquired a wealth of information when the most prominent names in various world literature movements are concerned. And then, at a late stage in my life, I have discovered the written art of William S. Peters, Sr. Not even once since did I resort to my old inclination of putting only those renowned writers on a pedestal of widely-spread societal judgment. I now had a most notable collection of literary writings on my desk, those composed impeccably by the author of *Eclectic Verse*.

Soon after my initial familiarization with the poetry of William S. Peters, Sr., I coined the term "Williamesque" in reference to his writing style. (No relation to Shakespeare, sorry!) The author's diction, form, imagery, content and context stood out uniquely among those multitudes of poets, essayists, storytellers, novelists, dramatists, playwrights and creators of other forms of prose, whose works I had analyzed over a large number of years in painstaking detail. Peters is a writer to be acknowledged on a world-wide platform for the groundbreaking elements he introduces to mainstream literature at large. His early fascination with words of all etymological origin is evident in the voluminous compilation of over fifty book-length publications under his name. It is, however, not a mere fascination that is of mention here. He speaks words into life. And while he does, he offers his readers, poets and non-poets alike, a wealth of information in this art field. The delivery is not forced, however. Once perused closely, the entire body of the author's creative writings comes to clear view as being representative of a highly sophisticated model of instruction on poetic composition. Peters' written work at large demonstrates his innate talent for creating verse effortlessly in an assembly of words that are spoken into life, voiced uninhibitedly through inspirational content and rich imagery, and a masterful embrace of the offerings of form.

At this point, a fact needs to be clarified succinctly: William S. Peters, Sr. is not an academic, nor does he ever pretend to be one. This introduction piece is purely based on my own analyses of and interpretations on his poetry at large. Putting it simply: He has a natural gift.

In *Eclectic Verse*, we witness William S. Peters, Sr. deliver his poetry in his conceptualization of form as a multitude of possibilities, serving content of symbolic and of literal context masterfully. In the tradition of his previous fifty+ books, the author traverses also in this collection multiple poetic domains, among which the following stand out: *irony, synesthesia, transcendentalism, anaphora, invocation, conceit, apostrophe, cultural criticism, allusion, imagism, paradox, deconstruction, anthropomorphism* and *complaint* – not about a hopeless love, as conventionally done but rather of satiric in nature, directed at the ills of social justice. Peters makes frequent use of genre-specific techniques as well, including *deep image, enjambment, cadence* (including *vers libre*, i.e. *free verse*), *circumlocution, assonance* and the *triadic line*. His writing style encompasses the methods of Ethnopoetics, Conceptual, Confessional, Didactic, Objective Correlative and Prose Poetry, with a few visits to the makings of an Occasional Poem.

The impact of Peters' poetic composition is compounded with a wide range of evocative content throughout *Eclectic Verse*. The metaphors he instigates accentuate an intellectual origination point and thus characterize the philosophic 'conceit' as esoteric overtones; he intersects genres into visual modes in the service of expressing a "self" at a heightened level of consciousness; he does not shy away from repeatedly voicing self-revelations; he incorporates entities of the past and the present as far as their problematic history in his cultural critique, but projects on a hope-filled future of joined knowledge and harmonious change, and he also critically assesses the traditional canon under the light of an eclectic blend of interpretive strategies that incorporates on a cross-disciplinary base the fundamentals of psychology, anthropology, sociology, gender studies and old and modern history, thus subjecting largely overlooked marginal entities to a close examination. Moreover, Peters enables the reader to witness how language prompts meaning for a text, stressing the provisional nature of such meaning; through concrete images and experiences, he generates poetic meaning for his transcendental narrative, in which he molds the realms of the spiritual and the physical into a connect, while allowing an interaction between corresponding sense modalities, and he skillfully adopts situational 'irony' and 'paradox' for the majority of his poems in his articulations of a truth. And then, there is 'imagism' the author implements in a most exquisite manner. In those instances, he distances himself from his familiar diction and meter, transforming concrete images into colloquial language with apparent ease. The outcome is a masterful symphony.

One trait that is dominant in the author's writing style must be emphatically stressed at this point for clarification: His intentional abandoning of capitalization rules for the first person singular subject in the nominative case in his spirituality-laden poems. This seemingly idiosyncratic characteristic of his written word has been integral to Peters throughout his writing career with the aim to achieve also an outward distinction between the empirical and metaphysical "self". In sum, he speaks from a level of higher consciousness.

In its entirety, *Eclectic Verse* is yet another masterpiece by William S. Peters, Sr. His offerings on each page are the evidence. Enjoy!

hülya n. yılmaz, Ph.D.

Retired Liberal Arts Professor, Penn State
Published Author
Literary Translator
Ghostwriter
Professional Book Reviewer
Director of Editing Services, ICPI

Foreword

As children of the 1950's, we were taught to hide emotions and feelings and to outwardly display "political correctness". A poker face was your protective shield and exhibiting emotions equaled weakness. *Eclectic Verse* belies this theory.

From the first word, Bill opens a kaleidoscope of feelings that dwells within all of us. Every verse picture unleashes memories and experiences that are common to us all: The wonder of children, the depth of elders, the bliss of love, the pain of bereavement, the disgust of greed, . . . *Eclectic Verse* takes you there.

Bill's words evoke conversations with the ancestors:

> "As I barter the gift of their wisdom in exchange for my time and ear."

The complexity of mature love is examined as he emotes:

> "My love for you is greater than my fear of me."

I shall carry these words in my head as I moonwalk through my life.

Fasten your seatbelt and prepare for an honest, a raw, starkly accurate, revealing and totally relatable ride.

Thank you for this cleansing emotional soul shower, Bill.

Linda Alexander Henderson
Willingboro, New jersey

Eclectic Verse

mommy i hear those whispers . . . (again)

william s. peters, sr.

The Poetry

Eclectic Verse

Wonder . . . Conformity?
(Please read vertically where applicable)

I	Just	That	Our	Doing
often	what	have	"here"	"now"
wonder,	are	transcended	are	
	all	before		
	the			
	souls			

We do understand that "energy"
Cannot be destroyed,
It just transmutes
To dimensions
We have yet to fully comprehend
And therefore, yet to . . .
Embrace

It	That	But
is	is	that
not	expanding,	of
the		our . . .
universe		consciousness

So, I ask again,
What are they doing
In this moment?

is as is each and every moment.

for time is the illusion

of ourselves

that rests itself on dissolving

                                          This moment in creation

                                              It is devoid of time,

                                          in which we take stock

                                  and create our personal esteem

                                                  foundations

of "knowing" . . .

But I ask . . .
What do we know
About tomorrow,
Save our shallow perceptions
Laced with the wisping fabric
Of expectation,
A place where dreams
Become . . .
Necessary?

Well . . .
there   is   no   more
at this time
for   me   to   write,
for
I
hear   . . .   . . .   "Wonder"

whispering . . .
whispering . . .
whispering . . .
my
name

A Dimension Apart

There are moments
When "Profundity"
Takes a peek into our consciousness
To see if we are awake,
And if we are not,
Her twin sister . . .
"Revelation"
Keeps her mouth shut

There are times
When "Compassion"
Tickles our hearts,
Begging us to come and play with her
In the playgrounds of humanity,
And we shun her,
For the time at hand,
We mistakenly surmise,
It is not our problem

These things
Are of the spirit,
Which always prevails
Throughout time
Over the machinations
Of Man's thoughts
And inclinations

You would think
We would have learned
By now . . .
But sadly,
We are still but children,
Stumbling along the same path
In the garden life-scapes
Of our "human" expression . . .
If you can dare call it that!

Eclectic Verse

Our civility has to be bargained away
For a supposed life of leisure
And dreams of opulence

We forego our blessings
Of divine cognizance
That we may cling to the illusion

What does it take
To awaken
That we may understand the dichotomy,
The difference
Betwixt the finite,
And that which is . . .
Everlasting?

No! It is not about your religion,
Nor is it about the iconic figures
You edify
To give your life meaning

Truth is so much bigger
Than the messengers,
Yet it is a simple premise

It matters not the name you call,
Or who stands at your altar
Where you worship

No! Truth, the unimpeachable truth
Of existence
Has only one name,
And it cannot be uttered
By a tongue
Of this world,
For this world
Vibrates in

A dimension apart,
As does at times
Our heart,
Our consciousness

12 Years a Slave

It has been nearly 12 years
Since you have been gone,
And I have been a slave
Ever since
To many things

You were a slave in love with me,
And I was too

1 up . . . Can You Hear the Music?

Maladies and vices,
Crosses and Christs,
A myriad of things
Designed to entice us,
Yet we are the only
Ones that can suffice us
Once we let go
Of empirical devices

I sit and I ponder
About things I know not
Perhaps I did,
But I simply forgot
In the meantime, there's fear
They tell me, Hell is hot
So, you might as well live life
Giving it your best shot

Many sit on their asses
Waiting for gifts,
Praying to heavens,
Begging for shifts

Unburden your consciousness!
Give your soul a lift!
If that don't work for ya',
Just smoke yourself a spliff!

The trick to the matter
Is to learn to let go,
Step out of judgement
About life's show!
Don't get all wrought up
Or your top, you'll blow
Nurture your garden

And watch yourself grow!
It's really quite easy,
When you step to the side
Let the crap slip past,
Be not denied!
Uncover your light
And no longer hide!
Then, you will wonder
Why those years, you cried

So, along the path
As you presume there's an end,
The most cherishable trait
Is your ability to bend
Put the best of you forward!
To your inner heaven, send
Your reflective lights within
That they come back again!

1 up . . . can you hear the music?

A Poem for Mary

By chance or fate,
   We came about
      To know of one and other

I could feel her suffering
   Suppressing her light,
      Her joy,
         But we cannot allow this
           To endure,
             For sure

There is work to be done,
   That of the heart
      Which instructs the soul
         Along in its journey

Mary knew this,
   Mary is from that time
      Where we, the people
         Do this

To lament
   Is but a moment,
      Like a star
         In the heavens vast,
           Shining,
              Giving of its light
                 Where it may

Mary is like this,
   Even through the pain
      Of her own,
         Which at times

She does own
    And denies
        In the streams of
            Concurrence

I write this poem
For this servant Mary,
For she is a warrior
In spite of it all,
She answers the call,
Regardless the cost
And the pending
Seeming loss-es
She must face

And in the face of it all,
    She is still Mary,
        Standing tall,
           Resolute
                Without refute . . .

She is a poem
    To be recited,
        Cited,
           Sighted
                By those who would see

Cinderella
For those who would call themselves a Christian

He has insulted our women,
And the same can be said
For the men of color . . .
African Americans,
Puerto Ricans,
Mexicans and more

Not failing to mention
Islam,
Palestine
And every other damn thing he tweets,
Or that which proceeds out of his foul mouth

In the multitude of words there wanteth not sin: but he that refraineth his lips is wise. ~ Proverbs 10:19 KJV

Not that which goeth into the mouth defileth a man: but that which cometh out of the mouth, this defileth a man. ~ Matthew 15:11 KJV

A good man brings good things out of the good stored up in his heart, and an evil man brings evil things out of the evil stored up in his heart. For the mouth speaks what the heart is full of. ~ Luke 6:45 KJV

The heart of the righteous weighs its answers, but the mouth of the wicked gushes out evil. ~ Proverbs 15:28 KJV

But the things that come out of a person's mouth come from the heart, and these defile them. ~ Matthew 15:18 KJV

"Loose Lips Sink Ships" . . .

His ignorance is astounding,
To say the least

Like a 40-day old pair of used underwear,
He reeks a stench
That is uncommon
To our civility
And to that of humanity

No, I did not say TRUMP,
Though you may say it is strongly implied

He has many followers
Who have something in common
With his deranged mind-set

So, if this offends you,
I apologize,
But God does not!

If the shoe fits,
Try it on,
And you may find it comfortable . . .
For you,
For many of us
It is time to go barefoot,
For I am not Cinderella

In the name of Christ!

. . . That We May Live

I hear the cries
Of the children

I lament the coming
Of those unborn

The canvass is colored
In tones of grey,
And the artist
Sleeps away
While the ticking clock
Knows no rest

The test of time
Is upon us . . .
Will hope,
Dreams,
And prayers
Suffice?

Will intent alone
Deliver us
And provide a healing
For all
The broken things?

The mirror on the wall
Fails me
And shuns my truth,
For I can not look
Deep enough within
To find that place
Where my power
Over circumstances
Resides

It hides somewhere
In the shadows,
Those that I fear
Without admission

Yes, we inherently
Are a noble sort,
But to actualize
All that we pine for,
Long for
And desire,
There is only
One thing
We must do . . .

We must die
. . . That we may live

I lay down my life that I may pick it up again, for 'I' have the power to do so! ~ The Christed One

I Am

I am but
A living word,
Expressing,
Waiting to be expressed

I am a poem
Discovering
Its self

There are many treasures
In the bowels of my vibrant heart
That are vying
To be free
From the vilifying tethers
Of appropriateness

I am unhinging
The doors of my beauty,
My soul,
And I will no longer
Lock my certifiable essence.
My divinity,
My humanity . . .
Away
In the dark dungeons
Of reason

Fear has no place
In this realm
Where spirit indwells
And calls . . .
Home,
For I am realizing
With absolute simplicity
That . . .
I AM!

No One

No one really knew
But a few
That she was always there,
Watching,
Observing,
The wayward ways, workings
And witchery of men

Yes, they have been infected
By the alien amongst them,
And should their ways continue
Their once brilliant light
Will be no more

They were fading,
As never before witnessed
In the six previous epochs
And this was their last chance
For their souls' redemption

This madness for things
And accumulation
Made no sense to her,
For Father had provided
All that was ever needed . . .
Yet, they possessed
An insatiable spirit
That wanted more

So, the devil
Created things

She pondered,
And could not help but smile
As she considered that

Some have heard of her lore,
But most believed her
To be but a myth

Crazed delusional souls!

Men neglected the primal truths
Of creation . . .
Balance,
Reciprocity,
Attraction

Yes, they were willingly writing
Epitaphs of perdition
And damnation
Each day
Upon the walls
Of their indifferent,
Insensitive hearts

She was crying inside
For a few millennia now
But never as voraciously
As this day
In time

No one expected her
To pull out her sword
Of righteousness,
But this was her charge,
For her Father
Had named her
Karma
And no one really knew
Who would be next . . .

No one

A Saba' Queen

From the land of Saba'
Was born a Queen
Whose spirit reigns
To this day

She heard of the lore
Of this
Wise King of Jerusalem,
So, she packed a caravan of
Abundance
With Frankincense,
Myrrh,
Oils,
Precious Stones,
And gold, and
Sojourned
To meet him . . . Solomon

She tested his acumen,
And he tested hers

His spirit was a wily one,
For he knew the names of
Angles, demons and devils

That was the gift
Granted unto him
By his Yahweh

And as they say, in the
Kebra Negast, she
Succumbed
To his trickery
And drank the water

She had wooed the wisest,
And he fell in love
Thus, she was bedded,
And he lay his darkly self
Upon her
And planted a seed
That shall never fail

In time to come, when she
Returned to Saba'
She, Sheba, birthed a King . . .
Menelik
And a dynasty
That shall withstand time
Immemorial

At the age of 23, he,
Menelik went for a visit
To meet his notable father
He was then offered the land
And the crown
In homage to the fruits
Of her, Sheba's, womb

Of course, as history
Made its course
Through time
He, Menelik
Refused
For there was a greater beauty
He envisioned

It was biblical,
Yet, to this day
Not spoken of
For that would epitomize
The rule of darkness
Over light

As Black always
Trumps white

They came from the West
In the years to follow
Seeking the treasures of the land
Knowing not
That the land is just that:
THE LAND

Who can own it?
Not I, not you
For we are but products
Of her grace . . .
Mother Earth

The riches,
The wealth
Is embodied
In our spirits

That is what the Saba Queen
By the name of Sheba
Taught
The wisest man
Of all

A Saba' Queen

Which One Do You Feed?

i peeked under the skirts
Of our construct
And i saw the unabashed nakedness
Of 'Reality'
Dancing in circles,
Frolicking in the grass
With Truth, Deceit, Light and Darkness,
Love and Hate,
Indifference and Compassion,
Charity and Greed.

i was a bit confused.
i asked my self,
"How could this be"?

Is this what 'Reality' is,
Or is it as convoluted
As i?

i, being challenged
By this disturbing sight,
Had to sit down
And ponder,
Inspect,
Examine,
Think about
This denial.

Was this an
'Epiphany',
Or just an illusion
Challenging me
To think outside
Of the box?

Eclectic Verse

What is going on, i mused.

As i sat in an
Agitated repose
Evaluating,
Deciphering,
Weighing
And Discerning
This glimpse,
This peek,
A small voice
Began to speak,
Whisper
Ever so softly
Into the ears
Of my disturbed consciousness.

The voice was soothing
And gentle,
Warm and embracing,
Yet firmly assuring
In its evocations.

i sensed something,
A presence,
An absurdative one,
That was greater
Than what
i had ever
Witnessed or experienced before,
According to my now faint
Memories . . .

This voice,
This presence
Commanded my attention,
And i could not divert myself
From it.

Was this the voice of reality,
Or something greater
And beyond
The context of
My perception?

Yes, i must admit
That i am but a
Grain of sand
Upon the beach
Of existence,
For in my past,
Everywhere i looked,
Creation
Seemed to expand.

Whenever i saw
The offering of knowledge
Upon the tables
That adorned my life path,
i voraciously ate
As if it was my
'Last Supper'.

Well, this voice that spoke
Superseded
My feeble and finite,
Faulty, flawed understanding.

i . . . my 'I AM'
Realized from a spiritual sense
That i was already consumed
As i submitted my essence
To the mesmerizing moment
Where i was swaying
Due to an unquantifiable
Inebriation . . .

Yes, i was drunken.

Beyond the beyond,
There was a distant light
Sitting daintily
In my horizon,
And i could hear it
Calling my name . . .
Needless to say,
i began to walk toward its
Lore.

The whispering in the mist
Became more prolific
And spoke to me,
Through me . . .
Of certain things,
Of my evasive familiarity
Such as
Duality,
Dichotomy,
Diversity,
And Deference.

'IT' said to me
That coexistence
Was an inevitable law
That was the very foundation
Of all of Creation.

This made sense.

This voice went further in
To explain to me
And my yet fully un-opened
Door of understanding
That one could not be
Without the other.

i asked,
"Is this like the story of the two wolves?"
And i felt a smile
Envelope my countenance . . .
The Voice said, "yes,
Which one do you feed?"

Musing

I met one of my fair muses this morning,
And she spoke to me about
The other side

She told me of the joys
Of true freedom
And the absence of angst,
For all souls
Accepted each other
As they are, were
And will be

There was no time
To speak of,
Life was like an eternal day,
For there was no need for sleep

My perspicacious wanting
Was overflowing
With a new knowing
That I was okay

A Visit with My Muse

My colorfully hued muse
Came by for a visit
With my heart.

As she crossed the threshold
Of my humbled abode,
I noticed the tears
Streaming down her face,
Pooling in my soul.

During our time together,
She posed questions
We are all too familiar with,
Such as,
Why does Man
Choose to treat
His fellow family
As it does?

We discussed
The propaganda,
The rhetoric,
The lies,
The ignorance,
The indifference
And callousness.

There were many reasons we cited
And tried to shine a light on,
But we sadly realized, once again,
We have been down this road together
More times than we care to remember.

She further went on,
Immersed in lament

About the illusions of difference,
Such as,
Religion,
Culture,
Gender
Politics,
Geography,
Culturalisms,
Language,
Skin tones,
Cell phones,
Sexual persuasions
And a voluminous myriad
Of lists we create
To project our false superiorities
Over one another,
Making ourselves small,
Never to realize
That we are innately divine
And connected
By the same fabric
Known as humanity.

Oh, the insane profanity
We espouse!

All of creation
Resides in but
One house
Which none may escape.

My Muse became tired
And had to beg my forgiveness
As she excused herself,
For she could take no more
This day,
But I will leave
The door to my heart ajar

As I await the arrival
Of my colorfully hued muse.

Upon parting, she looked into my soul
And said: "Keep the hope alive!"

The Proof

I had this feeling
That I wanted to write

I had no topic
or a particular inspiration,
Yet still,
I felt compelled
To write

Much unlike talking,
One should only open their mouth
When they have something to say . . .
Or when they wish to eat

Then, there are those
Who open their mouths
Anyway
Just because they can . . .
I know a few politicians that way

Well, what to write about?
Writing?
Poetry?
Life?
Or should I reach for some eclectically
Obscure topic
And espouse some bullshit,
Vaguely relevant?

Perhaps, this is proof of
The fact that
I am a writer . . . huh?

Wow!

Mission accomplished.

Culpritiousness

his praelective propensity for pretension-ness
told me not to mention this,
but i have to anyway

his word-weaving wistfulness
was somewhat proclivitous,
and somehow, it made his day

to expand his vocabulary
though quite arbitrary
to find different words to say

what were his intentions
with the variable syllabic inventions
in his parts of speech and play?

they were but words,
suffixal, prefixal, absurd,
and they were not more than a display

there was no perniciousness
in his culpritiousness
his thoughts be not held at bay

Poetic Perspectives in Vanity

The other day,
I pulled out your poem,
You know,
The one you said was sooooooo good,
Awesome,
Spectacular,
Profound.

Well, I took it to the market
To barter
So that I could get a bag of beans
And a bag of rice
To feed my family.
The cashier looked at me
Crazily,
And called the manager.
He said to me
GTFOOH
(get the fuck out of here).

Disappointed,
Disheartened,
Disillusioned,
Discombobulated,
Just plain dis-everything,
I then tried to get on the bus
To go home.
I offered your poem
As payment for the fare.
The bus driver,
He laughed at me
And said
GTFOOH
(get the fuck out of here).
He then closed the door
In my face

And pulled on off
Down the street.

Walking home,
I thought about these experiences
And considered . . .
Perhaps, I should read your poem
To them . . .
So, I pulled out your poem
To read,
But . . .
I could not even read it myself.

Holy

You can build a wall
You can speak the words,
Filled with emptiness

You can claim the land,
But "She" shall never be owned
By the darkness

She is not yours
She belongs to the people
Who have walked upon her
Since the beginning of time,
For "She" gave of herself

We sojourned
In the spirit
And we were contained and held
Only by the hand of the Holy

One . . .

We once were one
A land of many tribes
A land of many cultures
A land of the people

Prophets have walked
And spoken of these times

Prophets have gone
And more are yet to come

Like Jericho,
The walls will come down,
For they cannot endure
The battle against the Lorde

We, the people of the land
Will trust in the righteousness,
And the land will again
Be liberated that all the people
May be nurtured by its spirit

Tribes . . .

We once were one
A land of many tribes
A land of many cultures
A land of the people

Holy
And that which is holy
Can never, ever
Be any less

Agendas

Everyone has one
Or more,
Whether subtle
Or profound,
Lofty
Or grounding,
Quiet
Or noisily sounding
It is 'self'
Upon the airwaves
Of our social fabric

We create,
We destroy,
We deploy
And employ

Oh boy! Are we not
Complex characters?

We create narratives
And rhetoric,
Consistently
Or sporadically
As we insistently
Seek to have our way
With life

We bring to the table
We all must eat from
Our joys,
Our strife,
Our rife
With life

We all have agendas
Some sweet,
Some sour,
Like processed sugars
At times,
"Sweet and Low"
Raw,
Agave,
Cane
And even some
"Splenda"

My God, this is inane!
Perhaps, insane
Or profane . . .
What was your name again?

But isn't life splendid
In how we rend it
And put it back together
In our attempts
To mold it all
To our own
Personal agendas?

Listen!

I am poetry
I am movement
I am consciousness
I am conscious poetry in . . . m   v   m   n
                                        o   e   e   t

Look at my
c
    u
        r
           v
       e
s

To do so, you must close your eyes
And
    d
       e
          l
             v
               e
In the wonder that you are
There, you will see me

My footsteps are light
They prance and dance
Across and through life's gardens,
Bearing naught but a delectable and sweet fruit

Taste me! I will bring upon your face
And your souls smiles that have no end . . .

Can you see me
Feel me
Experience me?

Embrace me!
For I am beauty personified

I am Poetry . . .

Listen!

Conditions

Children dying
All over the globe,
Greed running down the
Bloodied streets,
Scavenging for more

Vultures sitting on thrones
In palaces of ill intent,
Hawks serving their purpose,
Making the kill
So that they can feast
On the ignorance
And apathy
Of "We the People"

New weapons created . . .
For what purpose?
Don't we have enough?

In the meantime, there
Abides famine,
Disease,
Homelessness
And a myriad
Of not yet-named maladies,
Waiting to be created
By the demented ones
Of Big Pharma,
Government,
Global Corporations
Just to make more sales,
To have more power

The days of a champion are dead.
Now, we need Gods . . .
Yes, in plurality!

But not those of the flesh
Who vainly believe themselves
To be so

Propaganda seems
To be the new education module
Amongst the people . . .

Any new news? Huh!

Kleptocrats without tethers
To any form of morality
Are drilling holes
In the bottom of the ship
That we all must inhabit

Sooner or later,
They will start casting
Those they deem useless
Over the sides
Into the seas of perdition . . .

Oh, they started already?

Is Thomas Pynchon
As prophetic as
Orwell?

One can only hope . . .

The people need reparations
Do so and leave!
These are our conditions

Remember, remember
The 5th of November . . .

Medusa at the Gate

Hearts turning to stone

Cold stares from the right

Indifference abound

The sound of death

Ringing

From the evangelical steeples

But a Few Billion

A few billion more bullets
Manufactured today

A few billion more guns
As well

A few billion more contracts
Awarded for weapons
Against humanity

A few billion more dollars
Lost in trade wars

A few billion more acres of land
To be given away
For mineral rights

A few billion more people
Living in poverty, homeless

A few billion more refugees
Yet to come

A few billion more humans
Without food or shelter

A few billion more dollars
Sent out to space

A few billion more dollars
To create more disease

A few billion more dollars
Spent to look fashionable

A few billion more dollars
In tax cuts for the wealthy

Eclectic Verse

A few billion more dollars
Invested in Wall Street

A few billion more dollars
Lost

A few billion more plastics
Discarded in the wilderness

A few billion more trees
Cut down this day

A few billion more steaks
Grilled to perfection

A few billion more chickens
That can no longer roost

A few billion more poisons
Ingested this day

A few billion more
Cigarettes

A few billion more dollars
In medical expenses
That will not get paid

A few billion more gallons
Of oil stolen from Mother

A few billion more dollars
To fix Flint and the water

A few billion more dollars
For Puerto Rico's repairs

A few billion more dollars
For a valid education system

A few billion more dollars
Spent on vaccines that kill

A few billion more mothers
Who will lose their sons

A few billion more prayers
Sent to the heavens

A few billion more worshippers
Going to the temples

A few billion more tears
That find no solace

A few billion more
Distraught human beings

A few billion more
That lament the day

A few billion more
Praying for peace

Yet . . .
We spend trillions on War

A few billion more people
Who will turn a deaf ear
Or a blind eye,
For they live in a world
Filled with indifference
Until a few billion reasons
Come knocking
At their door . . .

It is time to put a stop to the bullshit!

The Aksum School

From 100 AD until 940 or so,
The Kingdom of the Aksumites ruled,
Schooled the lands known today
As Ethiopia and Eritrea.

They exacted tolls from the Romans
As they were roaming to and fro
From India and back again
Through the sands of Africa.

They had their own money,
For as Kush declined, they mined,
Minted and cast their own images
For the people to worship.

Before the days of the Christian,
They ruled, schooled the lands
With a firm stand of culture
And trade, so much that
The Persian Prophet Mani, who died in 274 AD
Regarded Axum as one
Of the four great powers of his time.

Of course, there was
Persia, Rome, and China . . .

Aksum, a place where the Ark of the Covenant
Is still sought, for they thought that the son
Of Sheba, Menelik brought it home
As a gift from his father, Solomon . . .

Have you read the Kebra Negast yet?

Under the rule of Ezana
In the 7th century,
Aksum adopted the teachings
Of the Christed One.

Muslims from Mecca sought refuge,
Fleeing the Quraysh persecution . . .
Their journey to the Aksum kingdom
Became known as the First Hijra.

Asylum,
You may have it,
For we are a civil people.

Welcome to the Aksum School!

Damaged

She was damaged

Continuously by her

Perspectives

Which came about

As a result

Of her selective electives

Whose correctives

Were beyond her

Detectives

She was damaged

And did not realize

The damage she was doing

Over and over to her guarded heart

and . . . i realize!

Naked i stand before Thee
In the temple of life
That no thing
May separate me
From Thee.

i bow my head in obeisance
Upon crossing the threshold
Of Thy temple,
Hoping that i may be acceptable
In Thy site.

At the altar,
i prostrate myself
And offer a prayer
For simple things.

i ask that Thy tears of mercy
Be showered upon me
And Thy brethren
And that we humbly,
Without knowledge of
Self-separation,
Bathe in Thy love.

Make evident
And let us know
Without equivocation
Of Thy blessed providence.

Let us be ubiquitously clear
And come to know
That we are one,
Have always been,
Will always be.

Eclectic Verse

Let me not come to depend
On the mind you have given unto us
To be the veil that shields us
From Thy glory . . . Nay!
Let us be without provocation
And discernment of Thy goodness,
For the ways of Man fail me.

i thank You this day,
As i am thankful
Every day
For Thy presence . . .
Seen and unseen,
Known and unknown,
For in moments
Such as this, i am clear.
For Thou, and Thou alone
Has allowed such a thing
To be realized . . .

And . . . i realize!

See . . .

Where is that place
Where dreams do come true?
Just open thine eye
And see now anew!

Thou have this magic
'Tis borne from within
Just believe, believe
Let the light show begin!

Hold to thine faith
That thou know of the way,
And together we can
Make brand new the day.

Open thine heart,
And thou surely shall see.
Let thy light beam brightly,
And the darkness shall flee.

Cast aside thy doubt.
Let loose thine fear.
Worry not dear soul.
Shed nary a tear!

Let us all join hands
With intentions a pure
And dance to a music
Not heard ever before.

Children of the world
Will come unto Thee
With joy in their hearts
Just open thine eye . . . and see

What have we to lose?

Independence Day

Did you say "independence",
Meaning free?

Wow, is it me
Or you who
Is delusional?

Our granted rights
Are being attacked,
As are many peoples and cultures
Who do not fit into the demographic
Of being like you.

Me? I have never been free,
Nor were my ancestors
Of recent memory.

You see,
The color of my skin
And various others
Who appear different
In some kind of way or another
Are ostracized from enjoying the fruits
Harvested in humanity's garden.

We have efforted,
We have toiled
And we have sacrificed
Our tongues to silence
While many of you
Embrace this thing
You call "Independence Day" . . .

Oh, what did you say?
What day do we celebrate the myth,
Fed to all of humanity
That we are free?

A slave to taxes,
A slave to fear
As you drop bombs,
Fire your bullets
All over our world.

Yes,
It is our world,
Afforded by creation for us all.

Oh, let me not forget to mention
Disease,
Famine,
Economic oppression,
Religious and cultural suppression
And our current regressions
Globally . . .

So, get over it!

Get on with it,
And let us together
Strive for REAL INDEPENDENCE
Not just today,
But every damn day!

Share your voice, will ya'?
Let us rise up
Out of the mire
The select few
Elect for us all
To exist in.

Rise up,
This and every
Independence Day!

And Shine . . .

Here I lay
the gutters of perdition . . .
With you, wings clipped,
Our wills spilled,
Third eye closed.

O tell me, dear brother,
Dear sister,
What have we come to?

The stench of our being,
Our humanity
Has long lost
Its inebriating fragrance.

Where is the bath house
That we may rise
And purge ourselves
Of ourselves?

Where be the new clothes
We must don
And begin
To once again
Look in the mirror
And reclaim our hope,
Knowing
That gutters are only
A temporary place
We lay in our search for solace?

Too much sleep did not
Bring us the serenity
We vied for.

"Trust in others
Who had agendas
To serve", they say.
Such was truly misplaced.
Was it not?

Now that we have,
In this brief moment in eternity,
Relinquished the reins
To our now-masters,
We must awaken
To cast off the shadows
That cloak our celestial
Countenance
To put on our robes of light,
And shine . . .
As we were meant to.

With Ribboned Bows

Her dress was pink.
It was pretty
Once upon a time,
But now, it was well-worn,
Aged, permanently soiled
With years of endurance
And a bit too small on her . . .

The pink had almost faded away.

There used to be ribboned bows
Scattered upon its bodice,
With lace on the hem,
But now, there are only
Tattered remnants
Of what used to be.

She and her parents
Were familiar
With hard times
Since the times
Of economic woes,
Put upon the people
By the ruling global class.

Yes,
They, the upper crust,
The elitists of her world
Enjoyed a life only found
In story books
That spoke of things
Relegated now to fantasy.

People these days
Suffered through
Their hunger

And lack of smiles,
Yet somehow
They found the innate strength
To move forward anyway . . .
By the grace of some God
Who has been absent
For far too long.

Jobs were scarce,
The road of life
Was rugged
And filled with an abundance
Of hardships.

Who knew the path
To happiness anymore?

But, somewhere deep inside her,
She remembered
When her pretty pink dress was new,
And that made her soul a bit more lighter,
For that is what she saw in her mind's eye.

Every day, she wore her pretty pink dress
With ribboned bows.

Beyond the Room
Inspired by my love, for my love and my love of self . . .

In the vast room
Of my mind,
There are many doors
And windows too
That I have yet to open
To let the light in

In this begging-to-be-unexplored,
Unconquered
And darkened room,
There are many corners,
Crannies
And crooks
That harbor things
I have collected . . .
Anxieties,
Doubts,
Worries,
Fears,
Tears
And other little queer nuances
That inhibit my potential of being

Let us not forget considerations . . .

That sounds a bit better
Than admitting to
My tethers
To my self-created, imagined kryptonite

So, ask me:
Why do I stay in my darkened room,
With all the doors and windows closed?

Sometimes, we have questions
We cannot readily answer about the light, don't we?

Some Day

Donny said,
"Some Day" . . .

I have been looking,
Searching,
Praying,
Waiting,
Hoping
And praying some more
That my eyes are open
That I may see such a time

I know not
Where the path begins,
For I dwell within
So, if it lies
Here in the world empirical,
Surely, I am lost

What is the cost
That I must pay,
If there is one?

Must I give my soul,
Or sell it to the devil
That I may walk
A level
And balanced gait
Through this experience?

I have known troubles,
I have known trials,
And tribulation
Has become
My best friend,
Always hanging around,
Looking to be fed

Eclectic Verse

By my despair
As I gasp for fresh air

It saddens me
When I look about
And see others
Who suffer more than I

Mine is one of a soulful thing,
And I imagine
That their plight
Causes much of the same

The same old song
Has been playing
For much too long . . .

The right, the left,
The right, the wrong,
Famine,
War,
Disease
And all other maladies,
Exacted in this fallacy
We call life

But I will forever,
Until my last breath,
My last heartbeat
Cling to this dream
That some day . . . !

Inspired by Donny Hathaway's "Some Day, We'll All Be Free"

Catalyst

In my coming,
Will you wait for me?

I have words
That are laced with thoughts,
Borne of the spirit
I was instructed
To share with you.

Some may be a tad bitter,
But I also have a flask,
Filled with the inebriating toxins
That will liberate your consciousness from things.

This elixir
Is sweeter than honey.

We, as ones who are
Connected to the whole
Will realize the common thread
That binds us to the whole of all.

Sssssssshhhhhhhh . . .
Listen!
There is but one word:
Love . . .
                         That is the Catalyst!

              Don't think about it, be it.
              Let my words be a catalyst,
              As is your very presence
                   One for me.

Things

Sometimes,
The things in life
Can be overwhelming,
But be not of dismay!
For your power over things
Is but a thought away.

It is often said,
"Change your thinking, change your life."

James Allen and the Christed One
Said, "As a Man thinketh" . . .
Wow! What can trouble me
If I do not think about it?

I once wrote a book or 2
Titled *Think on These Things*,
Borrowed from Philippians 4:8
I think . . .
Yes, it was.

Finally, brethren, whatsoever things are true, whatsoever things are honest, whatsoever things are just, whatsoever things are pure, whatsoever things are lovely, whatsoever things are of good report; if there be any virtue, and if there be any praise, think on these things.

Sometimes, I think too much,
And when I stumble,
I can usually attribute it
To either not thinking at all
Or my consciousness being
Turned off,
Distracted,
Or sleeping.

Most of the weeping
I have done in my life
Has usually come from

The errant steps I took
Here and there . . .
With the exception of
My tears of joy.

Sometimes, "things"
Can be so demanding . . .
You know, like
The rent being due,
Our grades in school,
Our bills
Our career,
What other people think of us,
Our homes,
Our children,
Our parents
And our friends and peers.

We develop fears,
And sometimes, doubts
And trepidation
About "things".
Yet much of the "things"
We envelope
In the heart of our perceptions of 'Self'
Need not be embraced.

Many of these "things"
Are out of our control anyway,
Or we need not own.
So, why do we dance
To a music
We do not like?
Conditioning?
Mental and spiritual colonialization?

When we examine our lives
With a finite clarity,
The things we once thought
To be mountains

Are naught but mere
Anthills,
With annoying little ants
Crawling through our thoughts,
Gathering food
For the incubating larvae
Of our future.
Be it
Low self-esteem,
Anguish
Or the celebration
Of our lives
And our journey.

I did say,
"Be not dismayed,"
Did I not?
Something else I learned and borrowed
From Isaiah 41:10, King James Version . . .

Fear thou not; for I am with thee: be not dismayed; for I am thy God: I will strengthen thee; yea, I will help thee; yea, I will uphold thee with the right hand of my righteousness.

Yes, that greater power
Resides in you.
You are an integral part
Of the fabric of creation
And that of the infinite
And timeless expression
Of all that is eternal.
So, what is it
That can knock you
Off your rock
And balance . . .
Except you?

"Things" are but temporal
At best . . .

"Things" break,
Get worn out,
Date themselves,
Go out of style,
And get resolved.
"Things" pass,
And we remember them not.

Something else I hold to dearly . . .
From 1 John 4:4, King James Version . . .

Ye are of God, little children, and have overcome them: because greater is he that is in you, than he that is in the world.

Things

What good are gifts if you do not unwrap them? ~ krisar

Heaven

The twinkle in her eyes says it all
When she looks upon my face, I feel
My self glowing as I have never been before.

She is my heaven,
My refuge,
The place I seek
When my eternal soul
Feels out of sorts.

I remember her
And the essence of her being
From long ago-pasts,
For she was of "The One"
Who fashioned me,
Filled me with breath
And made my heart beat
With a wonderous
Concordance,
Just as she still does.

And dance, I still do
As I view
That magical twinkle
In her eyes.

Reminiscing my heaven . . .

Expansion
Poetry will never fail you. ~ Karama Sadaka

This is true. Yes, it is.

Poetry
Does not fail us,
But we fail Poetry.
We falter,
We stumble
In the gardens
Of our dreams over our
Indifference, doubts and fears.

Do you live a poetic life,
Filled with Joy,
Happiness,
Compassion,
Harmony
And Love?

Wherever I look,
There is Poetry!

When I look within,
I realize that "I AM",
And that, my friend,
Is poetic.

You are poetic.
Life is harmonic, melodic and rhythmic.
Can you hear the music?

The great composition of life
Calls for our instrumentation.

When a leaf,
Solitarily or in groups,
Falls to the earth
There is poetry in the movement,

The journey.
Can you see it?

The clouds drift languidly
Across the skies,
Playing poetic games
With the shadows they paint
Upon Mother's being-ness.

I listen in my "Here-ness",
My "Now-ness".

I listen
To the brook,
The spring,
The river,
The ocean,
And I hear Poetry
Streaming,
Screaming
My name
With loud whispers
To my soul.

Feel me . . .

I am vibrating
In multiple dimensions.
For the gates
That collect the toll
To the bridges
That we all must cross
Open only to poetic spirits.
For Poetry is the light
Of all humanity.
The movement,
The journey is Poetry,
Perfection personified.

Feel the energy
And allow it
To anoint the spirit
Of your life!

Poetry is blessing my life.
It lays guard
To how I walk,
How I talk,
How I think,
How I smile
And to all other aspects of my life
When I move 'Me' out of the way
And allow Poetry to remain infused
In my ways, my spirit
And all that "I AM".

I see Poetry in your eyes,
Pleading to be untethered
From the mundane
We all endure . . .
Needlessly.

Blink for me
A million times
And then by 5 times 5 exponentially!
See the wonder of Poetry
That patiently awaits
The opening
Of your third eye!

Let us expand our horizons
That we may see our potential,
Looming with open arms,
Ready to embrace our
Evident evolution
As we resonate in verse,
Be whatever the form.

Eclectic Verse

Poetry is formless
And of form, it is
As you like it,
But like it if thy will.
For it is our collective destiny,
Fateful in nature.
For we were fashioned
By Poetry's hands
In love.

Expansion

Neque Fiduciam

Confidence,

I have none in our current leadership

The constant banging

Of his head

Against the wall

Has no purpose

Other than his pain,

For no one

Can hear the sounds of the blood

As it slowly trickles

Down . . .

Bathing the mortar

In the cracks and crevasses

Of the Wall's bricks

With his anguish

Critique

The pool where tears were spawned from
Was beginning to empty,
And the eyes which shed them
Were beginning to grow weary
Of all that they have witnessed
In this life-time.

It seemed as if
There was a virus abound,
Infecting the reason of men
And women too.

Children no longer had a dependable path
Available to them
That led to a balanced adulthood,
For the ones who were responsible
For their charge
Were maligned by
The discordantly skewed ways
Of the world.

Oh Lorde, what are we to do?

People of color
Being attacked
For being colorful,
For standing out
Because of their melanin
Which is proudly on display.

Yes, Black is beautiful,
But many see it as a threat,
A blight on humanity,
A nuisance
That disturbs their
False solace.

BTW, you are beautiful too,
Regardless of your hued-ness
Or the lack thereof.

Some would rather embrace
And project their ugliness
On our world
That could be so much more
Than what it is we see
Or tend to focus on.

When will reason assail
Where reason fails?

I have hopes,
As do my children,
My people
And my ancestors.

Can we not, some day, express
Our divinity
Beyond the errant trinity
You have indoctrinated us with,
Superiority, Privilege & Prejudice?

I have looked to your God,
Prayed to your God,
Cried to your God,
And there is no intervention
That brings a cease
To the demise
Or brings rise
To the deceased
Who have died needlessly
By your hand . . .
And continue to do so.

I must say . . .
It is not only I and we

But many across the globe
Who suffer your indulgence
Of GREED.

There is of course . . .
Palestine,
Afghanistan,
All of Africa,
Syria,
Iraq,
Libya,
Sudan,
Darfur,
Soon to be-Iran,
Yemen,
All of Man
And those who have yet to stand
And rebuke your avarice.

This is not much of a movement in verse
But a terse critique . . .

I hope you read this
And reason,
Like a phoenix
Is resurrected
From its grave.

Not every poem needs to be about flowers and butterflies. This poem was written about Love and the lack thereof. ~ wsp

Inner Conflict

There is a tear
Or two,
Or there is perhaps
A river,
Waiting
In the corner of my eyes,
Hoping
To wash away my anguish
That I have collected
Over my life-time
And that which prevails
In these times of present,
But it is no gift I think . . .
Lessons . . . huh?

I have seen suffering.
I have seen death.
I have seen so much pain
That I have held on to,
Contained somewhere in my heart.

They, these tears
Of fears and loss
Are pushing the boundaries
As I pen these lines
And build them into verse
Which manifests
Into this poem.

As I write,
I acknowledge
That I am still evolving.

Shall I die in this moment,
Will the slate,
My life's chalkboard
Then be cleaned
Thoroughly
That I may write a new epitaph
To house my shadowed memories?

Perhaps, death is the friend
Of us all . . .
After all, there is so much of it around,
Conscious,
Physical,
And spiritual death.

My God, where are you?

I was told, taught
That you were within.
I was also taught
That you were above me,
In the heavens.
Therein lies my inner conflict . . .

Maybe now,
I will open the floodgates.

what may come

i drank the water
i emptied the glass
but it was still filled
with my wanting

to be sated
is a transient thing,
for we ever desire
for that which we believe
we have not

i was thirsty
i felt the pangs of hunger
and i attended these urgings
only to be met
once again
at the corner of the street
i traveled,
the street of 'empty'
that i paved with my
perceived lack
and induced despair

what may come of me?

how does one abate such things?

am i filled?
if so,
with what?

The Anatomy of a Poem
(Disclaimer: This is not a Sonnet)

What is a poem?

Many would say that it is
About the rhyme scheme.
You know, such things as
Shoe
And do
And you
On cue
And what you know,
And what you once knew.

Others would say,
It is about
Your iambic pentameter.
You know,
The footsteps of the beat
And your syllabic execution.
The feet, man, the feet!

Many would say,
Does the poem
Move me,
Take me away,
Allow me to play
In the poets' visions,
Their dreams,
Their hopes,
Their fears . . .
Will I laugh, smile
Or shed some tears?

Some look for messages,
And many of us poets
Have none . . .
Worthwhile sharing.

What happened to the poet's
And the readers'
Caring?

Was the poem
A throw-away
Or a stow-away
To read some other time,
One which we never quite seem
To get around to?

Was the offered poem
Endearing?

Did you find a line
Or a verse
That gave cause
For your swearing,
Tearing
Or fearing,
Today,
Tomorrow
And what may come?
Or did the poem leave you hanging,
Looking for that
Summation
About its position,
Stance
Or station?

Was the poem
Informative
Or just another
Expletive
You depleted

Eclectic Verse

When you almost
Completed
Reading
The humble words
Of us,
The struggling poets
Who search for words
To touch you
In a place of understanding?

After all,
We poets,
Like so many others
Mainly just wish to be . . .
Heard.

There are many aspects and
Endless possibilities
To what a poem may be.
Quite frankly,
There is not enough paper
In the entire world
To describe
Its poet-ential.

So, I will leave you with this:
My simple anatomy is
That a poem should kiss you
In a place
Where the Sun
Does not shine . . .
No, not in the accepted respect!
It should help you
To uncover
And to detect
A piece of
Your missing self
That you have put
On that now-dusty shelf

Of Spirit,
Consciousness,
Compassion,
Humanity;
It should help you see clearly
The insanity
We endure
While taking you pleasantly
Or tersely away
To explore
The possibilities
Of the beauty abound
Within you
Or without.

From the darkness comes the light,
Our courage is spawned
In the womb of our fright,
And wrongs are reconciled
By the 'right',
And each day
Is birthed from
A night.

May this humble anatomy
Serve my own plight
In seeking to write
Something meaningful.

Poetic offerings . . .

My verse is FREE!

Horizon

I live in a corral,
But beyond my containment,
Self-imposed
And otherwise,
Lie possibilities
Yet to be explored.

I try my best
To leave the gate open,
For that which lies beyond
My 'Here and Now'-consciousness
Is whispering my name,
Beckoning me
And enticing me
To come for a visit.

I have ventured before,
Many times, to the land
Of the unknown,
The unseen,
But there, within its breast
Resides a daunting thing
That challenges my empirical self
To let go.

Should I?
Could I?
Would I?

I will some day again . . .

Soon, I think.
For I am but a wanderer
Of the spiritual sense,
And my incessant wonder
Has never been sated

Nor abated
By what one would think
To be a fated
Expression of being-ness.

I have waited
Most of my life
To know of the absolute
Where the courage existed,
To embrace a higher truth,
Beyond that which I perceive,
Believe or conceive.

Wait a minute,
I will be right back.
I hear the horizon
Calling my name . . . again
This time, with a sense of urgency.

Damn, I Am Awakening!

She smacked me hard in the face
Of my consciousness, and my third eye
Began to water . . . profusely

The tears flowed
Without impedance
And started to wash away
The variable illusions
And filthy delusions
I embraced tightly
As my truth

Damn, I am awakening!

A bright light
Gave cause for me to squint,
For the sudden onslaught
Of my forgotten brilliance
Was more than I was prepared
To look at,
Or face
All at once

I thought . . .
Damn, I am awakening!

My soul began to move
Within its self
And untethered me
From the finite things,
And I saw the universe before me
Begin to come to life and bud
In my private garden . . .
And yours too

As the sacred flower of reality
Blossomed and opened its petals,
There was a sweet fragrance

That permeated my awareness,
I became cognizant
That I was so much more
Than what I held on to
All those years
As a once-verifiable existence

My being-ness was expanding
And the music of One-ness
Began to become audible

I asked my self:
Was this music always playing,
Was I deafened by the pollutants
Of life,
The noise we, humans produce
In the recesses of our
Self-created darkness?

I said to myself . . .
Damn, I am awakening!

Now, as I was becoming
Consciously cleansed,
I began to vibrate
And resonate
In harmony
To a previously unknown
Non-empirical energy
That was opening doors of insight
And light,
Showing me a way,
Heretofore obscured

Dimensions were flowering
And yielding fruits of sweetness
That I could enjoy
At will

I Affirmed

I was more awake
Than I had ever been

I felt whole,
I felt perfect,
I felt strong,
I felt powerful,
I felt loving,
I felt harmonious,
I felt happy,
I felt healthy,
I felt wealthy,
I felt wise,
I felt my "I Am-ness"
I felt complete,
For I was!

This all happened
In a flash
When "Love Uninhibited"
Smacked me hard
In the face of my consciousness

A Poem for the Dead

There are things
I should have said
That are still in my head,
My heart,
My spirit,
But now that
You are dead,
I can only write these words
Hoping they are read . . .
By you

I wish that I said
"I Love You"
A trillion times more,
And for sure, you would still
Have to be here
To hear them

So, here I am
With this sentiment,
Meant for you,
Still floating around
In my heart,
My head
And my soul
Which has a hole
That misses your presence

You were a present in my life
Which ushered forth my present,
But know that I still feel your presence . . .
What a gift!

I am happy where I am,
But it more than likely

Would not,
Could not
Have happened
If it were not for you
And all that you did,
You do
Still to
This day, even in your
Physical absence

My Horror

We look upon the pictures of horror
That we are inundated with
Every day.
Yet somehow, we
Can resume our lives
With no apparent heaviness
That motivates us
To action.

I am damned mad,
And this madness
Is consuming me.

I think of the wars
The children suffer,
The diseases we have made
In the laboratories
Of misguided demons . . .
Our unfounded vitriol
Toward one and another.

Leaders, anxious
To drop bombs
And push nuclear buttons
Of divisiveness . . .

To what end, I ask.

All my life,
Terror was just around the corner,
Waiting for an opportunity
To strike.

What is this prevailing illness
That is consuming our mentality,

Eclectic Verse

Our souls,
Our reason,
Our hearts?

It is much more than
Hate,
Racism,
Greed
And the other infectious,
Viral bacteria
That has moved our hearts
Beyond compassionate recognition.

Demons are amongst us,
Bearing crosses, ankhs and words,
Telling us they know the way
To greatness
And salvation,
But they lie
As they have always done,
Always will.

Darkness does fail.
Just watch and see!
Our horrors
Of war,
Disease,
Hate,
Racism,
Indifference
Will be vanquished . . .
In the blink of an eye.

Wait for the morning!
For joy will meet us there . . .

Dance Music

Her heart was terpsichorean in nature,
And the music of her soul
Flowed effortlessly,
Touching all
That abided in her presence,
People and things . . .

She was the epitome of loveliness.
Her nature exuded a joy
Most did not comprehend,
Nor did they care to,
For her very proximity
Brought a certifiable mirth
To their hearts.

Her countenance was soft.
Her fragrance was invigorating.
Her voice was mesmerizing.
Her touch was enchanting.
Her smile was enslaving.

Yes, she was a culmination
Of creation,
An emanation
Of the elation
Of the divine,
And she was mine!

She is my dance music.

Nez Perce

We did not label ourselves
As "Noble",
But we were an honorable people.
We were warriors
Of life,
Of the spirit.

We falsely imagined
That there was only
One Creator,
And He created us all
The same.

We prayed on it all
That we may be granted
An understanding
That exceeded our circumstances,
But it did not come.

The winters became longer,
And hunger prevailed
In our villages,
For our hunting grounds
Had been soiled
With the greed of the settler
And the avarice of the "Blue Coats".

We question now
If their Statesmen
Were that at all,
For the only "stately" thing about them
Were the lies they so freely spoke.

We are the Nez Perce.
We have lived with honor

Since the Buffalo came,
And we shall do so
Even though they are now
Small in number
As are we,
But we shall remain
Through all time
Nez Perce . . .
An honorable people.

In the Room

I come amongst you
From a land afar,
Yet close.

My tongue may be foreign
To some,
Yet, I speak a language
We all know.

I speak of such things
As our children, our wives,
Daughters, sisters and mothers
Remain in their subdued anguish,
As they suffer the workings
Of us men.

I speak of the need for more flowers
To be planted
To adorn the pathways
Of our hearts as we saunter
Aimlessly, meandering through
Our Creator's garden.

I ask: Have we lost our purpose?
Have we lost our connection
To that divine
That resides in the recesses,
The core of us all?

We are not quite lost yet, are we?
For it is evident that
We have gathered here
To share our humble words of spirit
And perhaps light another candle
In the room . . .

Fire

All men are born with a fire inside
A small flame, waiting to be fed

Many of us
Suppress its grandeur

Many of us
Let our flames burn wildly out of control

Many are not even aware
That such a magnificent characteristic exists

And many of us . . .

Disclaimer: The above poem is incomplete . . . I think.

No!

You cannot steal my light,
For it is inherent to my "I AM".
And, "I AM".

"I AM" the love I always wanted to be.
"I AM" the expression of what I see.
"I AM" the essence of what I "BE".
See my "I AM", and thus see ME.

"I AM" free from complicity,
For it is my choice
To do as I see fit.

No!
You cannot steal my light,
But if you feel for real
That it is light you need,
I have plenty.
For I have been freed
From the dogma
"They" feed us.

How about you?

Dysfunction

Since the death of my beloved,
The mother of my children
In 2006,
There has been an abiding
Disharmony betwixt us.

Who is to blame?
Is it God?
Cancer?
What?
Who?

The pain, at one time, was
Unbearable for me,
And I am sure
They too saw themselves
Facing unsurmountable odds.

They too had a hard road to navigate
With little help from my end,
For this experience
Was new to me
As well.

Perhaps, I should have studied more.

To this day,
In the absence of discourse
And discussion,
We have not come to any reconciliation
En masse,
But I continue to pray, love and hope
That there may be a light
That comes on
And brilliantly illuminates

Eclectic Verse

Our goodness of heart
And our unwavering capacity
To love.

They are good children,
Absent of malice.

They are intelligent,
Loving, compassionate
Gifted and talented
And so much more . . .
Yet, there still seems
To be something missing.

Is it faith in the process,
God,
Me,
Or themselves?

Either way, whichever way
The winds of the future bring forth,
Whether it be change or none at all,
I shall continue to pray that the light of
Dysfunction wanes
And that our joy
Will come
In the morning.

This poem is dedicated to all the fathers who endure dysfunctional relationships with their children, and to the children who must endure our lack of understanding.

Mantra
My Daily Affirmation

i am whole
i am perfect
i am strong
i am powerful
i am loving
i am harmonious
i am happy
i am healthy
i am wealthy
i am wise

i am because you are
because we are one LOVE

i am beautiful
i am blessed
i am charitable
i am faithful
i am grateful
i am kind
i am yours

i apologize
forgive me
i love you
thank you

her story

A Collaboration between Leslie Ann Roman, AKA "Mizz Fab" and William S. Peters, Sr., AKA "just bill"

(just bill)

her story
    was a hard one to read
but it is a story
    that must be told
so, pay attention

        her story screams like the front page of the news

        not just status quo, her story is unique

        custom-made through blood, sweat and tears

her tears run like rivers
    ever constant, down her face
she faces them
    and embraces them as her own
for it was told to her,
    and now it is known to her
that she is the cause of her new truth
    life told her she was not worthy

(Mizz Fab)

    people told her she wasn't gonna make it

    she ignored it but it was still engraved on her heart

    in her soul matter

    so even though she was strong and surviving

    she felt like a nobody

and even when no one saw her cry

she let tears pool

she would wash herself of all transgressions
  'til she felt whole
but she never could be
  'cause this stain-glass window
was composed of pieces
  and each fragment she held inside
was an exquisite figure
  which shined brightly
when she let the sun in

(just bill)

yes, she was broken

at one time, long ago

and her life had no rhyme

nor reason

and season after season

she spent tryin'

while cryin'

pleasin' others

only peekin' within

to see if she was whole again

relationship after relationship

affair after affair

Eclectic Verse

    love-making session after love-making session

      but love was not found

we all know that life is not fair, don't we?

she pleaded with God
  that his Staff and His Rod
    would either end this misery
      or fix it
but that shit did not work
  for it was
    her work to do
      not His

(Mizz Fab)

    and they say a woman's work is never done

    but she was tired of always being on the run

    helping out everyone but herself

    and somewhere, she had gotten lost in fairytales

    'cause the good guy never showed up

    as for all other people, they just didn't care

the bruises on her soul were fresh
  more tender than the physical ones
and she cried out for someone to hear her
  but nobody listened
so, she screamed
  and still nobody listened
so, slowly she started scribing her story
  some chapters, written in blood
some chapters, written in tears

as each chapter formed
   in front of her eyes
     she began
       to heal
         she began
      to evolve
    into
a wonderful woman

(just bill)

and then came along
   another Prince Charming
      flexing his ego
while arming, loading his
   weapons of mass destruction
      that could not heal her
for he never did feel her
   all he thought about
      was himself
and all he did for her
   was bring forth
      a wealth of confirmation

                she saw him as the affirmation
                  that she was worthless
                    as opposed to more
               and when she went to hide
            inside of her inner closet of doom
                 you know, that room
             where our inner child resides . . .
              she touched something sacred
      where all the tears of her years of her soul bled

                 they met her at the door
                 and began to conjure
                     transformation
                  and to her elation
                 she recognized finally
              that she was so much more

she was beautiful
and all her scars painted a picture

she reached into her soul
and found an amazing woman living inside
she opened the door
and the windows

she let the sunshine in
and had much to smile about

she was still safe
behind the walls

she let the light shine through the crack
breathed it in
let it into her presence
and knew that even if
the world fell apart
she would still be alright
this was life
and the speedbumps
would hurt
but she would make it
all she had to do was believe

                          with her struggle
                                 with self
                            she discovered self
                        and all its gloriousness
                          she found her own light

(together)
                This is her story . . . what is yours?

This poem was composed impromptu for an event themed by Leslie Ann Roman, titled "Her Story" to bring focus on domestic violence and abuse in November 2011 in Springfield, Massachusetts.

The Internet

It brings people together
From near and afar,
By plane by boat
By bus by car.

Small conversations
Can lead to dreams
As we vie to escape
Our present means.

Cultural differences
Are put aside,
And possibilities forward
Are deified.

We pray, we hope
For what come may
That we'll get together
Some near distant day.

Some are blessed
To loose their tethers,
Some are blessed
By love's fair weather.

The tender embrace
For which we all long
Is worth believing,
For love rights all wrong.

We anxiously look forward
To that very first kiss
That leads us to
Our garden of bliss.

Eclectic Verse

Yes . . .
This net connects us
In ways naught before.
The potential is endless,
When we walk through its door.

Black Hole

There is a black hole

At the center

Of my "Blackness"

That is sucking away

All of my dis-ease

This universe

That I now inhabit

Called 'my life'

Will soon cease to be . . .

Me!

Silently Dying

We are silently dying here,
Lending not our voice
To the change
That will eventually come,
Even if we are not here . . .

Will you get left behind?

Perhaps when we,
The un-blossomed flowers
Are gone,
And the weeds
That have cooperated with us
In the garden,
Choking away our life,
Have died,
Our footprints will remember
How lightly we walked
Through our lives,
Leaving behind
An essence,
Devoid of
A humane or divine character.

The time is always . . .
NOW!
Or, will you acquiesce
To the ways of the . . .
Silently dying?

Everybody Hurts

Her heart was continuously embraced
In her grief
This is why she had kept
Its doors unopened

He was not much better off
Than she was,
But he veiled his grief
With a false sense of bravado

The truth of the matter is
Pain, a deep pain
Resided within them both

What was the cause of such a thing
That stole their light
And their life, daily and nightly?

Even their dreams were haunted
By their lamentations and anguish

Was it an errant word,
A gesture or a fear that most possess
Because of this world
We have learned to endure
And callously forgive
With no tethers to a consciousness
That seeks resolution?

I often question
The seconding of my suffering
Of heart . . .
In the end,
I would rather love
And be misunderstood

Than to not have loved at all
Yes,
I will leave behind
This false sense of pain,
For its burden
Is too heavy
For my heart
To carry any further

Pre-Historic

We came before what
You call "history"
Was ever recorded,
But we were not savages.

Our civility was that of our own
And sent forward in time
That you may have a basis
To claim your own place in time.

We travelled the oceans
Which meant
We had means
To do so.

We fashioned vessels
To hold and cook
Our fare,
And we ate.

They call us now . . . "Lapita"
What is this but a term you now use
To categorize us, encase our evolution
In a frame of time, from 1600 BCE-500 BCE . . . ?
Yet, we live on,
Even to this day.

We gave many of the Pacific Rim
Language,
Art,
Pottery
And the understanding
Of ocean-faring,
For we understood the heavens
And all that was within them.

Eclectic Verse

We navigated
Through all aspects
Of life with a heart
Of reverence.

We founded islands,
And unlike those of you
Who came after,
We did not lay ownership
To the uninhabited,
And yet, we did not claim
This as our own.
We just coexisted
With what was given to us,
For . . . we are
As you call us,
"Lapita".

We came before your history.

. . . are mine to find

i have chased butterflies
and impregnated dreams
in the fields of my Lorde

i have seen days
when the longings of my heart
and the thirst of my curiosity
could not be abated
nor sated

i have tasted the bitter fruit,
the un-ripened
and the sweet as well,
and each bite
had a divine story to tell

i have experienced
elated thoughts
that i never believed
would be,
could be
grounded again

i have uncovered
and exposed
smiles upon the faces
of children
and adults alike

i have shaken hands,
shared ideas
and broken bread
with those whom i thought to be
strangers
who thus revealed unto me
that we were kinfolk

Eclectic Verse

i have found a certain solace
in the quiet eyes
and gentile ways
of the elderly
who blessed me in barter
with the gift of their wisdom
in exchange for my time
and my ear

i have walked
the wonder of the field
and the wood,
and was introduced
to a realm of existence,
a wonder about me
i / we often ignore

i have seen
pink skies,
blue skies,
red skies,
grey skies,
yellow skies,
white and purple too,
all with this wonderful
pair of eyes
that share their joys
with my heart

i have stood naked
and unabashed
in torrential rains
and the soft alike,
and felt a deep cleansing take place
in my soul
as my entire essence
was purged of the stains
and soiled feelings

i did not readily wish
to let go

there have been many a mountain
in my life
many, i passed by
some, i climbed
of which many i did not crest
nor put forth my best effort
yet just the same,
i am still the richer
for the experience
of trying
and vying
to see if i can

i have laid upon my back,
daydreaming,
musing,
watching the clouds of those skies
as they watched over me,
and we played together
a game of "Shape Shifting",
becoming something other
than what we were

i have stood on many a beach
and looked out upon the vastness
of a seemingly endless ocean
with my toes dug in the wet sands . . .
and the soft beached waves
caressed my feet,
whispering tales
of far-off lands,
far-off beaches,
far-off sands
that are a part of my horizons
and my "Here"

Eclectic Verse

i have spent days,
putting aside duty
to indulge
in the wonder
of letting go
while daydreaming
for no particular reason
or with any agenda

i was free

i have spent much time in my life
studying . . .
me,
attempting to see
what else i could be
or what was wrong
to see what kept me
from singing my life-song
clearly
that which i dearly
cherish

there have been some answers
and many perhaps, i did not hear
but life continued with its agenda,
its venue of progression
and i could not stay in the past
no matter how much i tried,
for "Now" always reminded me
of what was important . . .
being "Here"

i have been extremely blessed
in my life

when i tire
i rest

when i hunger
i eat
or i fast

when i thirst
i drink
if i can

i can smile
or not,
but most importantly,
i can choose
so, i do
choose to be happy
here
where all these magnificent possibilities
and life options
. . . are mine to find

I Always Dreamed of . . . You

As delicate as a rose,
She spreads her petals before me
That I may partake in her fragrance
And the presence of her essence

She blossoms
In my consciousness,
Opening new venues for my dreams
Of what may be and become

I rise each day
With a fervor of expectation,
For I know that she will be
By my side

Through our discussions,
Our embraces
And the glances of affection,
I am enhanced

My journey has led me to this wonderful garden,
And I am deeply appreciative for all the inclinations
That led me down the paths that I once viewed
As errant in nature . . .

But can that which is of nature
Ever be wrong?

So, here I am,
In this magnificent flower-garden,
Immersed in a goodness
I always dreamed of

yes, i dream
dedicated to all of the mis-diagnosed children of our world

                                                                   dreams filled my head
                                            tumbling and running around,
                                                            looking for,
                                                                seeking
                                      a crack in my consciousness
                                            so that they may escape
                                                  into the realm
                                                        of reality

                        i did/do not mind them at all,
                             but sometimes they, we
                               are quite the distraction
                    that gave/give cause for me to
                             forget the tasks at hand

some people may call this
an 'attention deficit disorder',
but for me
it is a realm of being
that brings me more joy
than this world of things
i was stationed in

                         you wanted to give me medicine
                                that i may sleep,
                                a dreamless sleep,
                  but there is naught whatsoever wrong
                          with where i choose to be

                                              the mundane,
                                         the rote-filled,
                                         the rites of life
                        and the demand for acquiescence
                                      and conformity

                is quite the challenge,
                whose purpose appears
                   to keep me from
                     the 'beautiful'

in my dreams,
i can conjure,
create
astounding,
magnificent,
scenarios,
dimensions
that perhaps you
no longer understand
since you have grown up . . .

                but my only prayer is
             that i will forever be filled
                  with a wonder
             that transcends this reality

won't you dream with me
of a better tomorrow . . .
a better **TODAY**?

Forever

The darkness came around the corner,
Stealthily creeping,
Attempting to encroach
Within the boundaries
Of my divine shine

I have never had to draw a line before
But now, I see it is pertinent to do so

The man-made clouds
Are being spread across
The landscapes of life
In the fields,
The playgrounds,
The hills,
And the meadows
Where we, children, play

But know
That your consciousness
Is yours to command
So, demand
That the demonic shadows
Flee before we really
Light up and vanquish the darkness
Forever

He Had Been Stripped

He had been stripped
Of all the things he possessed,
All the people in his life that he loved

The memories faded
Into that void of
Oblivion

It is then that he found . . . his self
Lying in the murky bottoms
Of his self-created abyss

His light was dimmed . . . deliberately,
For he was not ready and willing
To come to grips with his truth

He looked upon him-self,
Mired in his anguish and self-pity
And the very act
Of directing his
Consciousness
Upon himself
Shed a light
Upon the shadowy regions of his soul

He was found
By "Him-Self"
Within "Him-Self"

She Walked Leisurely

And languidly,

Provocatively

Into my consciousness

Her feet, filled with mud,

Leaving evidence

Of her visit

Upon the White Persian Carpet

Of my supposed

Unstained perspectives

I was forever changed

Just Like You

We tie our shoestrings
Just like you

We drink from cups or hands
Just like you

We eat our fare
Just like you

We think,
We feel,
We cry,
We smile
Just like you

We vie just like you
For the essentials of life,
Such as food, shelter, safety
And the nurturing of our children
And all the other comforts that life affords

So . . .
Why do you treat us as animals?

Is it because
We do not appear just like you?

Bliss Knew My Name

I had been a hard-working Soul for quite a long time. It has been a while since I took a Spiritual Vacation. I thought about this often. You know, sometimes you just get tired. Though we may rest on a daily basis, there is most certainly an accumulative weariness that has a profound affect upon our spiritual persona. Yes, I needed a vacation.

I really did not know how to go about this. Whenever I take a break for my Spiritual Pursuits, it leads to no good. What is that little saying I used to use . . . "by design or by default". Well, my Spiritual Hiatus was just that: "by default". This time, however, I was keenly aware of my need for a break. My question was just what should one do to exact such a period of rejuvenation that I felt i direly needed.

In my examinations, the first thing I decided to do was take a personal Spiritual Inventory. Just what exactly was the issue? What was it that I felt . . . in truth, besides tired? In all honesty, this was one of the most difficult tasks I have ever had to undertake about "Self". I found that there was an underlying and prevailing guilt beginning to arise as I contemplated stepping away from the essence of how I defined my "Self". Interestingly enough, I found my 'self' down on my knees in meditative silence, seeking answers. That was not good, because doing so only served to remind me of just how tired I was. It seemed that this path was well-worn and I needed a refresher, yes, a big refresher!

In my contemplations, I examined my joys, you know, the type of things that brought abandoned smiles to my Spirit; the type of joy one has for no particular or objective reason. I reached back into those memories I had stored over the years. They came in quite handy as I contemplatively examined their characteristics looking for that special light that I equated to a sort of "Self-Liberation" . . . Yes, that was it! I needed to be liberated from Self! I had for long, I think, been liberated from such things such as societal indoctrinations and propagandas, however there still seemed to be some sort of an ominous rote-like essence infecting me at a deeper level. And now, it was showing up.

A funny thing began to happen as I went deeper and deeper within in my search for that solution to my Spiritual Quandary. I saw this light . . . no, it was not incandescent, nor was it fluorescent or of any other reasonable explanation of all that I have known in my past. And I am quite familiar with the usual revelatory type lights that come to consciousness through deep meditation, or what I call . . . "Zoning". This light seemed to also bear with it a feeling, a glow that enveloped not only my consciousness, but it overtook aspects of my 'self' that I did not know existed, as I felt this warm, enveloping wave of deep peace. It was sort of orgasmic in nature, but much more complete, for it had no vibration, no peaks or valleys. It was like a continuous embracing wave of Bliss. It is at that time when I heard

Eclectic Verse

"The Voice". I would like to say "The Voice" was of a feminine dynamic, but that would be my feeble attempt to define and characterize that which was so much more. This was more like a melding of all that I was into a complete state of true "BE"-ing. And though there were no definitive words I can remember being uttered, this is what I was residually left with upon the cessation of this episode:

"Child, I am who you are. We are of the same ilk, the same source, we are pure energy. I am that which sustains thee, as thou are what sustains all that I am. I exist simply because you do. Our co-existence is completely symbiotic. In your quest for peace, understanding and joy, you have activated your deepest power, and thus being summoned, in obedience to the Will of that which is Divine, 'I AM' here . . . now. I am Bliss. I am that elusive energy who peeks into the lives of Man from time to time. Though I am yours to command as your are mine as well, our relationship in the 'Know' has left much to be desired. As a matter of fact, you have turned your Spiritual Back to me, seeking things in the world of illusion to satiate that which you always possess within. Many nights and days, I have cried for you. Yes, I am that dull ache you feel deep within your Soul for completion. Yes, I am that longing for 'Home' your heart so often speaks of. Though I am gladdened when you connect with each other in the Heart Zone, I need you to know that there is so much more that you need to remember. You take on burdens and you call that 'life'. You have allowed your Celestial Mind to be enslaved to this slow and dense vibration, and somehow, you have come to enjoy it. That deluded aspect of illusion and ether you now identify as 'Self' is but a wisping shadow of your Greater Being. Remember, shadows are but evidence of light . . . but they are NOT LIGHT! You in your essence were created from, by and for light . . . be that which you are. Radiate. In truth, there is nothing that can contain your possibilities, except your own Divine Consciousness, and with that, you have done a masterful job. It is time for you to let go and let your Source Creativity come and enliven the Soul Dreams you held secret for all these eons. You are as the Stars in the Heaven, and I pray that you come to the realization that you are the Light of the Cosmos as are your Brethren you witness in the Night Sky. They have always been there to light your path back to your True Dreams. We all, your Cosmic Family have been waiting for you to embrace your 'Knowing and Is-ness' again. We ask you to believe and have Faith in your Soul-Path. Find your Rest in Me. I know you and you know me, and your name is . . . Yes, I am your Bliss, the One you seek, and I know your name."

meop sdrawkcab eht

deredro eb tsum ti taht smees efil
dnatsrednu nac ew taht
sredrob eht txiwteb stsixe efil taht
dnamed yb dehsilbatse

epacse ot gniyrt ma i tub
etor dna etir lla morf
os robal od i yhw si hcihw
eton elpmis siht etirw ot

Take on the challenge!

Thorns and Storms

She was as pretty as a
Blossoming Rose
At the height of
The Spring season,
But her heart had thorns

As beautiful as a
Rainbow
After a warm summer's rain,
Yet her sky was adorned
Still yet
With clouds
That spoke of
Storms to come

Was it circumstances
Of the past
That caused
Her anguish
Her mis-trust
Her fear
Her vitriol?

Did she have doubts
About her ability
To love
And
Be loved?

She is like most of us,
But we are the unspoken expressions
Of our silently soiled souls,
For confronting truth
Is most times
A daunting thing

So, we pretend to be
Roses and rainbows
And be damned
The thorns and the storms

Afraid to love . . .

I Will Not Be Chained

I am the spirit of
Queen Nanny,
I am a Moor at heart
And I will not lie down,
Sit down
Nor stand for
Anyone to attempt
To enslave my
Body,
Mind,
Nor spirit.

My Soul is FREE!
And the 'I' in 'ME'
Shall follow
The path
That my Father
Has laid for me.

There are many chains
About . . . no doubt
Be it Religion,
Taxes
Or the nexus
Others wish to perpetuate
To contain my divinity.

I was birthed
From the womb
Of a people
Who were of color
In so many ways
And that shall not end
Regardless
Of the days

And these times.
You attempt to
Perplex us
With your sexist,
Tyrannosaurus Rex-ist
Ways,
But as my Grand Mammy told me,
"You can never be enslaved
Without your consent!"

I did not know what that meant
Then . . .
But now,
I understand
I am a man,
And only I
Have the power
To alter that stature.

I am a Moor at heart
And I shall not part
From my ways
Or that of my Ancestors
Who rebelled

Some allowed this sentiment
To fester . . . within
With an inner resent-ment,
Meant to quell
The spell
Of the whips and chains
Which still remain,
But . . .
But I,
I am FREE,
And I will not be chained!

Forward Reflections

I dipped my quill
In the inkwell
Of tomorrow
That I may scribe
Of the promise to come . . .
My hopes,
My desires,
My wanting,
My dreams,
And my longing.

There was a mirror,
Formulated within
The words and verse
I penned.

When I looked
Deeply in the reflection,
I saw none other
Than my self
Looking back at me
As it awaited
My becoming.

Forward reflections . . .

Oceania

The waters had their lure.
They whispered to us
Of undiscovered horizons.

Perhaps, if we meet the Sun
Either where it rises or sets,
We will see the glory of its womb . . .
Or perhaps, we will fall off of the edge of existence.

Let us build us a vessel
That we may travel
Beyond our meagerness!
And perhaps, just perhaps,
We will discover
Something grand
In the looming Oceania.

home . . . come

there is a flame
that burns
in the deepest recess of my heart
and it burns for you,
waiting for you,
lighting your pathway home

the child within me
sits in solace,
quietly praying
for your safe return
that i may hold you again
in the embrace
of the Holy

the Angels dare not make a sound,
for the reverence
of this sacred moment
which holds all eternity
calls forth but a word,
a voice only God himself may speak,
and we await pensively
for that utterance of praise
when the Bride and her Groom
are reunited
in the chamber of matrimonious union

as my Brother Solomon once said,
"thy breasts, my Love, are comely,
and I long to lay my head
and listen to the universal rhythms
of thy heartbeat
as it speaks and confirms
the truth of our oneness"

images of long ago,

sweet memories
still dance
and dominate my thoughts,
for consciousness
of your "here-ness"
is all i desire

so long have i longed
to feel thy gentle touch
upon the skin of my reality
that it may dispel these delusions
yes, delusions i have created
to keep me company,
delusions that you
have never left me

i had to deny this truth
to maintain my sanity

it is not vanity
but my "vain-ness"
that does adorn the wall of my house,
that which whispers questions,
offering a confirmation
while seeking an affirmation
that i do deserve thee

but truth of the Light to be told,
"I NEED THEE"
to complete me
and fulfill the cup of my dreams
that i may drink again
from that fountain of love
borne in the Womb of Creation,
in you

i have kept the lantern of hope burning,
for surely, if i am not diligent
darkness would consume me . . .

again

i abide in this whirlpool of convolution
with my loins afire,
with this burning desire
and a relentless passion
that again we will consummate
our union
before the throne
which is seated
in the Garden of the Divine

this is the Sweet Fruit,
that of a Soul fulfilled,
where the Harvest is never ending

and thy sweet nectar of bliss
shall again drip
from my lips,
and you shall feed that need
for me to plant my seed
of the divine

i shall plant them
in the furrows of thy goodness
the "IS"-ness
where the Children of Sovereignty are borne,
spawned in spite of
that which comes
to claim the hopes of Man

and i, a Retired Warrior
now sit in this Silence,
listening for your footsteps . . .
i know them well,
for each footprint of anticipation
is indelibly etched in my heart
as i sit here

on the edges of sunshine,
cloaking myself with dreams,
visions,
prayers
and other supplications
to Creation
and He who holds all things

i keep this Flame,
for i am the "Keeper"
of that "Eternal Light"
within me

and each heartbeat,
each breath
confirms that it is so
as i await your presence
your return
home . . . come

erat scriptum

thus it was written
that the time shall,
and a child shall lead them

sic passim

it has been spoken before

and once again

the voice shall be heard,
chanted unto our souls
until our recognition awakens

i auditis prius vocation
hoc est, conscientia nihil
expectantes est cor meum
hoc ipso realization
quia ego adsum
in quo ego mihi semper fuerunt

sede
audite
et voces
quae parit ratio
quod sonat
iterum atque iterum
sonanti
verba, quae et transcendit tempus
et puer parvulus minabit eos

The Life of Death

When the leaf
Began its new journey,
Cascading through the air
As it fell from the limb
Of the tree,
It was not death
Within its embrace
Nor its destination,
But that of a new life adventure,
For it would go on
To become the nurturer
Of the soil
That feeds many roots,
Many trees,
Many limbs,
Many leaves
Who will
At some time
Also embark
On a greater mission
Of expression
As that of this leaf

The Life of Death

Bless Up

I know not whether a tree sheds a tear or laments that of the loss of a leaf or a limb, but I do.

Here I Am

Today, I am grateful
As I was yesterday,
The days before
And the days to come

I have been watered,
I have been fed,
I have been taught,
I have grown
Beyond my expectations
And imaginings . . .

I have been nurtured
By the Universe, by Creation
And the fragrant hands of my Creator

Through the essence of the design
Of ALL that exists,
I have come to this realization

It is . . .

That His works,
The Universe
Has ALWAYS
ALL WAYS
ALL DAYS
ALL NIGHTS
ALL TIMES
Provided me with 'enough',
For here "I AM"

Sure, the road may have been
Very trying at times, but still . . .
Here "I AM"

Singularity

I climbed that mountain
Named "Glory"
Where "Blessing"
Lived upon its peaks
And speaks
Of the wonder
Of all creation.

The struggle was arduous,
But my soul was not familiar
With defeat.

I scraped,
I clawed,
I fought
And I weathered the storms.
I endured
By the grace
Of my Creator

Finally . . .

As I stood upon the precipice
Of my achievement,
I looked upon the valleys
From whence I came,
And I saw
Greater things before me.

Is life not beautiful?

Endless possibilities . . .

Open thine eye!

Singularity . . . to thine self be true!

I Am Grateful

You are my paradise
You are my refuge
You are my safe, warm place
Where I can rest my weary soul
From the toils of the world

Though I too have days
Where clouds loom above me,
I know that somewhere
In my humble existence,
Your sun is shining brightly,
Waiting for my arrival at consciousness,
And your brilliance
Is always with me

All I need to do
Is open that third eye
You have adorned
Who I am with

You are my paradise
You are my refuge
You are my safe, warm place
Where I can rest my weary soul
From the toils of the world

I am grateful

What Percentage of Human Are You?

Christian, Muslim, Buddhist, Hindi
Or other . . .
Who is your God?

Do you hold tight to the tenants
Of your faith
Or just mold them
As required
To justify
Your small perspectives?

Reflectively so . . .
Though I was born without a choice,
I am a Christian
So they tell me . . .

Why, you may ask . . .

Well, it is like this:
My mother, my father
And grandparents
Were Christians.

Not so sure about my country . . .

But I, did not have a choice,
Did you?

So, when we examine
The rudiments
Of our declared faith,
The prevailing question is simply this:
What percentage of human are you?

Christian, Muslim, Buddhist, Hindi
Or other . . .
Who is your God?

Muse

She seemingly surreptitiously slithered

Silently into my solace-soaked

Consciousness,

Tickling, stimulating

My wonder and curiosity

She wanted to play,

And I wanted to sleep

But that would not be,

For she had a poem

She wanted to give to me

I am waiting . . .

Sumerian

I am the culture you now embrace
As your standard.

I have given you insight
To the meaning of
Your guttural utterances,
For I created
The written language.

Are you civilized . . .
Yet?

We, from Sumer
Invented,
Created,
And imagined
A progress
Of no end,
And
Here you are,
Trying your best
To do so . . .
End it . . .
All.

Hear our call
From the annals of time,
For civilization
Is the last paradigm
That matters.

Strive for it,
Embrace your humanity,
End the insanity
Created . . . by your inane
Ways.

A message from the Sumerians

How Could I Forget Her?

She etched memories upon the consciousness
Of my heart . . .
Daily.

For ink, she used a combination of
Tears and blood, infused with
Mirth and love . . .
To make it permanent.

How could I forget her?

Her pen was her sword.

Words . . .

Powerful they were!
For I can recite even now
Every cutting syllable
She spoke
With her tongue
And with her eyes.

How could I forget her?

Though I speak
Of my convolution
In love,
Know that
It was all worth it,
For she was a healer . . .
She always nurtured me
Back to my perfectly happy self.

I would have it no other way!

How could I forget her?
She was love
That which I strive to be . . .
Daily.

How could I forget her?

Breathe

These hills are mine and thine,
My laddie!

Our fathers
And our father before them
Have nurtured these lands
With their blood
Sweat
And tears.

There are more years to come
Than what we have spent
Holding to the promise.

We have tilled this land
With purpose,
With a certain freedom
Throughout
Many a season,
Many a year . . .
Raised our stock,
Our children
And our families . . .
This is your inheritance!

Can you not hear the music
Of our forefathers
Dancing,
Playing in between
The whispers
Of the winds?

O laddie,
Just close thine eyes
And open thy heart

To the way of the Scots
And feel your Gay-like,
Bonny,
Bright,
Gaelic
Blood coursing
As one
With us, the people
Of these highlands.

Breathe!

Who We Are

In a world
That appears to be
Abundantly filled
With errant things,
Errant ways
We must learn
To choose different paths

The crooked cannot prevail
Over a spirit
That is determined
To walk a straight path

Lies
And deceits
Can not prevail
In the light of the absolute . . .
Truth

Broken hearts
Do heal
If one but
Removes the locks
And opens
Its doors

Delusions
Wash away with the tides
Of reality
When they come to visit
The shores
Of "Right Consciousness"

Fear cannot stand
And defend its self
When one acknowledges
Their own autonomous divine power
Of eternity

Doubts are but the children
Of courage
That inspires one
To look in the mirror
Of the soul
And embrace
One's bigger self

Be encouraged,
For all will be all right-ed
With the passing of time

The rotted fruit
Shall be rendered
Into a sweet wine
Of experience,
And we will become
Inebriated
By that, the Omni-essence
Of who we are
And by that which has spawned all things . . .
The Primal!

The greater Light
Will not come to you,
Nor will it visit its self
Upon me,
For it is already here
As it has always been . . .
Here within
Who we are!

Neither shall they say, Lo here! or, Lo there! for, behold, the kingdom of God is within you.
~ Luke 17:21 (KJV)

Although the Supersoul appears to be divided, He is never divided. He is situated as one. Although He is the maintainer of every living entity, it is to be understood that He devours and develops all. ~ Bhagavad Gita Chap 13, Verse 17

In the Midst

In the fold of noise
That seems to envelope
Our consciousness, there is a silence
Calling to our souls to listen

In the busy-ness about us,
There exists a place where stillness prevails

Can you feel it?
Breathe it in!

Seek it, and you will
Discover once again
That place from whence
Your soul was spawned

The dawning
Of the new age
Approaches . . .
Will you awaken
From this tangled nightmare
Where deceit and illusion
Rule the day?

Naught of the empirical
Is everlasting,
Save that
Which lies
In the midst,
Awaiting your presence
Once again

The Sun Always Rises

Know that shadows
Always follow the light . . .
Be the Light!

It is easy, I say.
Let go of the thoughts
That seek to define
And thus contain you!

Darkness does thus flee
When you allow your
Soul-shine
To come out and play.

You are the product
Of a magnificent creation,
And a magnificent creation
Is fashioned
By the hands of
Your Consciousness.

Be the divine!
Yes "BE"!
Now is always
The right time.

Just remember,
The Sun always rises.

Let us rise and shine!

Bengali

We are a people.
We are a land.

We speak in a language
Of diversity,
And have done so
For many a year.

From Bangladesh
To West Bengal,
We exude many colors,
Many tongues
Many means
Of worshipping
The Creator
Of all things.

We were once called
The Vedda from Sri Lanka
And later, we embraced the
Mediterranean peoples
Who spoke Indo-European languages . . .
We did not mind,
For they too
Became one of us,
For we were strong.

In the 8th century, we welcomed
Peoples of Arab, Turkish, and Persian descent
As they migrated
To our lands . . .
We embraced
One and another
And called ourselves
The Bengali.

Today,
We stand
As one
For one,
For us all.

I Wonder

I wonder what Tupac would rap about
Today
I wonder what Harriet Tubman would do
I wonder what Frederick Douglas would
Say
I wonder what X
Would speak on . . .
To us . . .
To you

Let us not mention
Nat Turner,
His dissention
And how he turned history,
His-story
Into a blind narrative
Of denial
Without the trial
Of truth
And justice

Is it just us
That continue to suffer
The buffer
Put betwixt truth
And reality?

Swimming in the Mud

                                                                              Swimming in the mud

Is a challenge

                                                                              That any fish like me,

Like you

                                                                                 May not overcome

Sometimes, in our lives

                                                                               We feel as if we are

Swimming up a hill.

                                                                                Without the assist

Of a flowing river

A Prevailing Mindset
Dedicated to all the people of color who condone and support the current racist and fascist regime.

Massa',
Please pat me on my head,
Smile my way,
Tell me once
That I have done
A good job

I know that you may see me
Unworthy,
And not an equal,
But I will pick yo' cotton
And yo' tobacco
Until my fingers bleed
From sun up
To sun set

Massa',
Please pat me on my head,
And smile my way . . .
I just want to please you,
For I do not want
To taste the sting
Of yo' whip
No mo'

Massa', please . . .

Our First Time

Was like an eternal time
That we have shared in that moment
When I looked into
The endless love in your eyes

You were searching me
Deeply
Looking for the level
Of my sincerity

Divinely Flawed

I live in a world of poetry,
Words,
Inspiration,
Love
And . . .
Energy

My medium is words,
Which I so love,
Study,
Create, Kwee-Ate, Qweate
And seek to hone
That I may convey
The beauty
And other
Of what I see,
Or at least think I see

Everywhere I look,
When I look,
I see poetry
Dancing,
Prancing
Lifting her skirts
That I may get a peek
At the undergarments
Of truth . . .
Sometimes, they are absent,
And "Truth" nakedly exposes
All of her grandeur

Sometimes, I can bear it,
But most times, I cannot,
For "Truth" is stark in contrast
To the life that I live . . .

Mostly
My vanity,
My ego,
My delusion
And the illusions
Oft times
Shade her light
To look other than what
"IS"

There are many lights
With all degrees of brilliance
And a myriad of colors,
Many which are not detectable
By our empirical eyes . . .
Their vibrations are foreign
To our "Status Quo"

All of this
Comes not
Without purpose!

Flawed, I proclaim,
For in what name
Do I defame
That which is Divine . . .
Mine?

Father, forgive me!
For I too,
Know not what
I DO . . .

I must admit not
That I am "Divinely Flawed"
And thus, I am awed
By the perfection
Of it all

Eclectic Verse

My mind is imperial
And I subtly seek to colonize
My thought,
My experience,
My perspectives
To fit
Borrowed paradigms
That are not that of mine own

If you cannot be the poet, then be the poem. ~ Unknown

Paleo

We journeyed to the east,
Crossing land-bridges
That no longer exist.
Bliss was not to be found,
Save in our visions
Of a new life
In a new world.

We fashioned tools from stone
And trees.
We built our villages
From what Mother provided.
We educated our children
On our ways
And the ways
Of the land.

We were a reverent people,
Respectful of all the spirits
That nurtured our people.

We hunted, we gathered
And we found solace
In the horizons,
The sunsets,
The moon,
The rivers,
The mountains
And the valleys.

We multiplied our hearts
And our presence,
And the land welcomed us,
Embraced us
And fed us.

Eclectic Verse

We found civility
Upon this land
Before the times you now deem
Civil.

We had many tongues
And dialects,
But one voice
Which still speaks
To this day.

We are Paleo.

Conditional Love

Sometimes, you will encounter

A soul or a few

Who offer their hearts

To you

Circumstantially,

With conditions

Undefined,

Until you,

They

Find out,

Discover

Who they truly are

I Wish

I wish that I could
With the blink of an eye,
A wave of a hand,
A fleeting thought
Change the world
Into one big expression
Of
   Love,
Tolerance,
   Love,
Acceptance,
   Love,
Understanding,
   Love,
Embrace,
   Love,
Coexistence,
   Love,
Temperance,
   Love.

I wish . . .

Wishes do come true!
Wait on it,
Believe it,
Have faith in it
And work towards it!

Extend a hand,
Open your heart,
Allow your consciousness

To expand
Once again
Into the realm
From whence we came,
And where we are destined to return.

I wish . . .

Questions to Ponder . . . or at Least, to Wonder About

How long exactly is eternity?
How vast exactly is infinity?
When will forever ever cease?
How deep is the void we call abyss?

How sweet is that first kiss?
How warm can a hug be?
How insightful is one's third eye?
What happens when you die?

How dark can dark be?
From where are illusions spawned?
How bright can light become?
If you add nothing to nothing, what is the sum?

Does love itself have no end?
What is it that lies around the unknown bend?
Is there a limit on that which I may create?
Tell me exactly how I can learn of my fate?

Where does a "start" truly begin?
Can you tell me exactly, who decided what is sin?

Just a few questions . . .
Questions to ponder . . . or at least, to wonder about

Discovery

She brought out my magnificence
As I attempted
To bring hers about
As well

We felt compelled
To share this gift
Of each other
With the world

We journeyed,
We met many souls
Who beheld us
Whom we are beholding . . .
In our hearts

Yes, we love each other
And our sisters and brothers
As well

From land to land
And back to our homestand
We saw the sights,
The lights . . .
By day
And by night

We were embraced
By cultures discovered,
Uncovered
By the lovers
Of life

Yes, there was strife
But that did not stop

The children
From smiling . . .
And adults
As well

I cannot begin to tell you
About all
That we discovered . . .
Uncovered

We were witnesses
To the greater aspects
Of what humanity is,
Can be,
And is becoming

And all of this
Is . . . simply
Because
We danced
In our hearts
As we were enhanced,
As we strove
To discover our
Magnificence
And yours
As well

Discovery

The Letter

I sent a letter to
Lady Karma
And that Blind Bitch,
Lady Justice . . .

Hopefully, they
Will wake the "F" up
And do their appointed jobs.

I wrote this letter
With my sharpened quill
Of consciousness,
Compassion,
Empathy,
And need.

The ink was a special mixture
Of tears
And of blood.

I expressed the pain
We as a humanity
Are collectively suffering
By the hands of the few
Who think selfishly
Only about and in their
Grand delusions
And from the cortex
Of their
"God Complex".

This letter
Was the hardest write
I have ever done,
For I had fears,

Pain,
Exasperations
And frustrations
Because
I doubt
If anyone would
Read it.

But . . .
Just the same!

In the name
Of all that is Holy,
I penned these words
With an absurd belief
That it would make
A difference.

The Letter

Humanity

There is that pendulum
That swings
To and fro.
There is Karma,
And there is that law
Of reciprocity
That is universal
In all of its expressions:
Balance.

You would think
That we would have learned
By now,
But we are a challenged sort,
And we dare call ourselves . . .

An intelligent species

Humanity

Smiles

The Devil smiled at Faust
And walked away with his soul

The Devil smiled at the Christed One,
Proffering temptation,
But the consciousness of Christ
Did not yield

The Devil smiles every day,
For it is his nature
To disarm the unassuming
And hoodwink those
Who are not weary of his presence

There are demons and devils amongst us . . .

A Tribute to Love

There is a spirit that prevails,
Carries my warmth
And all that I deem worthwhile
Within her breast

She is my smiles,
My laughter,
My tears
And my
Happily ever-after

She is the wind
That makes my wings
Feel integral,
The soft breeze
That carries the fragrance
Of the blossoming
Of my dreams
Of the future
And that of my
Now-ness

She gives me purpose!

My prowess
Is enhanced
By her presence,
And I dance
Because of her
Essence

Her embrace,
The light upon her face
That leaks from her eyes
Staves off

Eclectic Verse

Any demise
That dares to approach me,
For she alone
Is my reproach
For the shade or shadows
Made in the meadows
That lie
At the feet
Of the mountains
I have come to climb

I think my self
To be a poet,
But she is my rhyme
And my ability
To envision
And conjure
The things of
Magnificence

Does that make any sense?

Well, it doesn't have to,
For I have her . . . love,
And in these lines,
I hope you too can find
A reason
To pay your own

Tribute to Love

My Truth

In the quiet stillness,
Just before the Sun
Peeks above the horizon,
My space is filled
With contemplation,
Inspection
And some . . .
Retrospection

There is a subtle anxiousness
That I project into
The coming day
Along with a healthy dose
Of apprehension,
Task,
Duty,
Verve and vigor

I ask myself,
What shall come
Of this time
I have been allotted?
What things are living
In the shadows
Of my
"Things to do"-list?

What have I forgotten to do
Yesterday,
Or put off until
This tomorrow
Which may never come?

Yes, in this quiet time,
Just before the Sun

Eclectic Verse

Peeks over
The horizon,
I hear the faint whispers
Of creation
Calling for me
To live
My truth

Such a Place Exists

In the land
Of far-away
Where life knows not
Of its potential
Nor the possibilities . . .

There is a village
Where dreams are underfoot
And wishes are cast
To the waysides
Of life.

No one aspires,
No one has desires,
For these such things
Have long ago proven
To be fruitless pursuits.

The skies were always overcast
And the woes of the people
Lasted . . .
To the point that there
Were no points to be made.

A dismal maid
Walked the earthen street,
No smiles apparent
Or within her,
Or anywhere
To be found.

She was but enduring,
Securing a place
Where she felt comfortable
To face . . .

Death
Life here was but that . . .
Death lording over the people,
Like the Fat Man
At the circus.

May mercy be upon us
That we never have to visit
Such a place!

Such a place exists . . .
Does it not?

Just look to the path we now walk on,
The things we talk about . . .

We shout,
We pray
The day,
The night
As we dwell with our blight
That we have allowed,
Or created.

One cannot be sated
With that which is hated.
Can we?

When I Die

Prepare a place for me,
Brother,
And I will for you.

We shall twinkle
And dance in our own light
Upon the canopy
Of the heavens,
The night skies
Giving light
Unto the wayward traveler
And the lost.

We shall point the way
To the men of the land
That they may accomplish
Their dreams
And walk with a surety
Across the heretofore
Unseen lands
Of their horizons.

Prepare a place for me,
My brother,
And I shall prepare one for you.

Let us be the light
Upon each other's path . . .

I Want to Be

I want to be
Your refuge,
That hole you climb in
When you need
A place of solace,
A place to hide out
When you do not wish
To face the world.

I want to be
That person you come to
When you need someone
To listen.
I do have two ears,
One to listen to the you,
And one to listen
To my internal voices.
For a while,
You can have both.

I want to be
The one
That lifts you up
Above me,
Hold your hand
Through doubtful times,
Be your rhyme
And your reason,
Season in,
Season out
As we go together
All about
Removing
All fears,
All doubts.

I want to be your dance partner
To hold you forever

In my embrace,
Tasting the sweet essence
Of your presence
During my journey.

I want to be
Your best friend
From beginning to end
And back again,
And again,
And again . . .

I want to paint smiles
In your heart
That will never part
And always fill you
With mirth,
Joy,
Peace,
And . . .
All the other virtues
Our existence
Has for us.

Let us trust
In what I want to be,
What you wish to be,
And together
We will see
Wonders abound
Surrounding
Our every thought,
Our every dream,
Our every intent
And desire
For a better world.

I want to be . . .

The Blood

The blood upon the pavement,
The streets
And in the fields has dried.

Its stains have faded away,
But the stench of death
Still prevailed
In the air.

It was not that of the people
Who were martyred for the cause . . .
FREEDOM,
But that of the soldiers
Whose souls had given leave
To their reason,
Conjured from the imaginings
By the deluded minds
Of megalomaniacs.

Power is a nefarious thing.
It is not all that
We think it is.

It is not the bullets,
It is not the stones,
It is not the bombs,
It is not the angry words,
Nor can power be found
In the souls of those
Who would lead us
Into perdition,
Those with an insatiable greed.

Power is in Truth,
And Truth is an inventory

Found in our closed closets
In the House of Soul
And in the bedrooms
Of our now-small, sleeping, troubled hearts.

It would seem that
Since time immemorial
Man has always sought to define,
Categorize,
Cache,
Bring to life
And focus on
That which divides one from another.

Is this the way
Of the children
Of the same Mother?

Our genesis is a common one
In nature.

Is this the path
That would deliver unto us
Our Utopic dreams
Of peace?

I have questioned my ways
Many days
In my "Now-ness",
My "Being-ness",
And there are many days
Which I would
Rather forget,
For I too can not escape . . .
Reality.

How are you fairing
With your self-induced delusions
Of grandeur?

Eclectic Verse

Do you sleep well
During your nights,
During your days?

The blood will be spilled.
That much is ever certain.

Will it be your loved one?
Will it be one you knew not?
Will it be that of your own?

I often wonder, how is it, why is it that the children can still smile. ~ wsp

Fire ~ Pyro

There was a fire burning within him,
One that he loved to throw gas on
Just to see how
The flames would burn . . .

Would they be high,
Would they be wide,
Would they move something
Deep inside
Of him?

He was not necessarily
A pyromaniac,
At least not your
Classic type . . .
No, he just liked
To see
The burst of energy
Raw fuel brought about.

Interesting,
How long it did not last . . .

Melancholy

She did not want much . . .
Perhaps, just
A little
Peace in her heart

She was lonely,
No friends of meaning,
A parent
Who was busy
With their own life

God never spoke with her
In a way
She could identify

Her life was relinquished,
Embraced,
And consumed
By her own
Inner hauntings

Sadness and melancholy
Were her best friend . . .
She could depend on them
To show up
Each and every day

They tucked her in at night
As she prepared
To once again
Dream of the void,
The abyss
Where flowers

Never grew,
Nor light
Ever shined

She wanted to dance,
But the only music she ever heard
Never resonated
Deep enough within her
To inspire her to movement

She wanted to sing,
But her heart knew of
No song

Smiles for her
Were disturbing,
Like enemies
At the gate
Of her consciousness
Seeking to destroy
Her solace,
The anguish within
She had become
So accustomed to

She did not want much . . .
Perhaps, just
A little
Peace in her heart
And a word from God,
Her Father
Or her Mother . . .
Either one would do

Melancholy

Pay attention to our children . . . they are the future of all that there is! ~ krisar

She ~ Her

She had a compunctious spirit about her,
And the question that loomed heavily
In the thick air around her . . . was:
"Was this character expression
Rooted in the core of who she was,
Or merely a rote-filled rite
She exercised,
Brought on by acquiescing
To pleasing others?"

Surely, she was not shining
As brilliantly
As she was capable of,
But she did not necessarily
Know that,
Nor was she keenly aware
At all times
That her innate magic
Was lacking

For far too long,
She was content
With the smiles of others
And their approvals,
Never realizing
That she was losing . . .
Her "Self"

She did not willingly
Choose this road,
Nor did she necessarily
Take responsibility,
But she did blindly

Go down this path,
Attempting always

To make the best
Of what she had to work with

Sure, there were joys,
Pleasures,
Happiness
And celebration
Along the way,
But there was always
This wearisome feeling
That at times disturbed her peace
As it whispered,
"There is so much more",
Or "why not me?"

She had become
Quite adept
In her ineptitude
At suppressing these faint voices
That lived within,
And somehow, she was always able
To reason them away

Her friends celebrated her deductive skills
And her intelligence
In a way . . . for they too
Were much like her,
Living not quite
Fulfilling lives

She found some sedative solace
In their pats on her back

Still, she prevailed . . .
As this inner restlessness
At times
Disturbed her sleep,
Or either carried her away

Eclectic Verse

From her "Now"
Into the lands
Of "Wishful Thinking"
And "Day Dreams"

She was not the religious type,
Though she prayed often
Nor was she particularly pious
In her outward life practices,
Though she did believe
Somewhere deep within herself
That there was so much more . . .
Yes, SO MUCH MORE!

As time went on,
Her life became more and more
Sedentarily solitudenous,
And she developed a false comfort
With the things
She had accumulated,
Her personal life achievements
And the life-expression-habits she embraced
In her abandonment
Of pursuing answers
To the questions whispered,
Uttered by those voices
That used to entice her
To have a bit of courage
Every "Now and Then"

She found comfort and solace
In her reflections,
Though she had long ago
Forgone
Any critical introspective examinations

There were only circumspective thoughts
With dim and dimming lights

That no longer illumined
Her wonder
Or questions
She remembered asking
In her youth

Yes, she had a good life,
But she knew the truth . . .
It could have been
So much more . . .

Had she had the courage
To live

To choose to live at one's optimum does not always take intelligence as much as it takes the courage to let go of what we perceive to be intelligence. ~ krisar

Going Forward . . .

No, I have not always been
Diligent,
Vigilant,
Nor prudent,
But my intent was
Always with me.

Yes, I wanted to eat of the
Sweet fruit
I witnessed so many others
Enjoy.

I have planted seeds.
I have tilled the soils.
Why, I even took part in
Enjoying the spoils
Of a good harvest!
But I did not always
Do the work
I felt I was called to do,
Could do.
How about you?

There was my avarice,
My slothfulness,
My thoughtlessness,
My carelessness,
And many times,
I just plain fell asleep
On the job.

The Gift

I have been truly blessed
In all aspects of my life

Sure, there have been ups
And downs
And much falling
To the ground,
But sooner or later,
I have always been able
To get around
To rising again
That I may begin
To start surmising again
In my uprising again
That I may lift my self
Above my self
Of the past

You see, nothing ever lasts,
And I have always been taught
That "This Too Shall Pass".
So, when I look at it
And center-consciously consider it,
Life is but a class
Where I have come to learn
And take forward
While paying forward
Lessons and blessings

Gifts are for giving

My Love

My love for you
Is greater than
My fear of me
That I might fail
Once more

It is that soft wind
That originates
From your heart
That keeps my sails
Billowing,
Filling me with hope
And expectations
For what tomorrow brings

I am singing
All the time
These days,
For your ways
Have taken command
Of my soul,
And I love
Your melody,
Your harmony,
Your symphony

Beautiful you are . . .
In all aspects

And as I said . . .

My love for you
Is greater than
My fear of me
That I might fail
Once more

We All Win When . . .

The children suffer our ways
In the days to come

Love is the way to the light
That all souls seek

Open thy heart,
Open thy hand,
Open thy mind,
And you shall find
Possibilities of peace waiting
To be spoken into the ether
Of creation and humanity

This day, won't you
Untether your ways
From that of the world
And embrace your divine self?

We all win when . . .

the grand charade

we apply our foundation . . .
man-made,
we put on our blush,
we color our lips
or gloss them,
we line the shapes of our eyes
as if they are not beautiful enough

Revlon, Maybelline and others
have convinced us
that our natural beauty
is not sufficient

we color our hair
spray carcinogenic chemicals upon our heads
to hold it in place

Perhaps this too is an incomplete poem . . . perhaps . . .

Indigenous

We stood upon the mountains,
Communed with the heavens
And spoke to Gods.

We built Pyramids.
We had medicine
Before it had a name.

We were civilized
Before the caves of western mankind
Were abandoned.

We understood nature
And what it required of us.

We witnessed ships come
From celestial places,
Spaces
Beyond your imaginations
As we looked upon the faces
Of Creators
Within every dimension
And beyond.

You cannot know us,
But we know of you.

We await your ascension
To your ancestral home
Where you too
Were once
Indigenous.

Thus So . . .

Her insightfully caring words
Soothingly caressed my consciousness,
Arousing imaginings
That were a bit warm,
A bit foreign,
But totally intriguing,
Enchanting,
Enjoyable
And quite mesmerizing.

I watched my self
As I hopelessly became addicted
To her love,
To love,
To the possibilities
She exposed
In me,
About me
That I once believed,
That ever loomed
Upon my horizon.
She actuated my now-ness,
That consciousness
I was not always
Keenly aware of.

Her smiles
Were like the rising sun,
Beaming brightly
In my heart.

Her melodic intonations
When she spoke

Awoke, awakened me,
The me of me,
And I embraced
The very essence
Of all of
Who she was,
Is
And shall ever become.

She is my present,
My presence,
And I now know
A bit more
Of the depths
Upon which
I am being blessed.

Life is a "Blue Moment"
When you allow

Thus so . . .

"Blue Moment" is a term borrowed from a story in *Small Graces . . . The Quiet Gifts of Everyday Life* by Kent Nerburn.

Lost

Yes, we were lost
In the same wilderness
As we still are
To some relative degree.

We are here,
Attempting,
Each in our own way
To find our way . . .
Home.

It is cold outside,
And our souls are hungry
For that warm, loving embrace
We once knew
And perhaps
Took for granted.

Oh, how I miss
That "State of Euphoria"
Which I can never forget
And long for acutely
These days!

I know that I am tired,
But I must push on,
As must you, my friend.

The briars along the path
Seem to reach out
To touch my exposed
And bare flesh
That they may leave
Scars and memories

Of this journey,
Of the lost
In my fortitudinous way.

No, I cannot give up!
I heard the whisper
That spoke so silently.
It said, "Son,
Just follow the light within."

Observing

It was a time
That was not quite
Understood

There were psychic
Movings,
Dancing in my thoughts,
Prodding my spirit
To awaken . . . keenly

Was I contemplating
Without subject?
What was my objective?

I sat, I listened,
I reached
For that elusive
Glistening epiphany

The realm of
Circumspection,
Introspection
And reflection
Gave unto no
Detection
In this state
Of abyss
Where naught but void
Exists

Was I seeking . . .
Bliss
Of peace?

Just observing

To Be

Or to be to BE,
That is the question,
For how can you not "BE"?
It is impossible!

Shakespeare had it all wrong.
Was he confused?

Guilt?
I cannot be that.
I will not be that!

Fear?
I cannot be that.
I will not be that!

Deceit?
I cannot be that.
I will not be that!

Hate?
I cannot be that.
I will not be that!

Yes, "I Am"
Love.
I will be that.

Compassion?
I will be that!

Thoughtful?
I will be that!

Conscious?
I will be that!

Eclectic Verse

So, what I be
Is up to me,
But I will always be
One thing
Or another!

My choice!

To Do

It was the worst of days,
It was the best of days,
Simply because . . .
I am alive

Don't get me wrong!
I am grateful for this opportunity
To witness
My hopes for humanity
To come to be . . .
But in the meantime,
There is so much
To do

To Listen

For the past couple of weeks,
I felt this deep calling

I tried my best
To remain observant
With a clear consciousness
That I may come to understand
Just what the message was . . . is

Is this the coming
Of a poem
Of profound proportions,
Or one of a particular delicacy
That needs to be acknowledged?

I am listening,
But all I hear
Are faint, indistinguishable whisperings
Here and there . . .

Perhaps, it is my heart
Calling for me
To do more,
Or to let go of the dark matter
That so often invades,
Shades our lives
These days

Yes, that must be it!

I look for God
In all places,
For I know that He / She / It
Always has a pocket full of pens
That He / She / It
May inscribe some meaningful verse

Upon my heart
Or my consciousness
Am I reaching?
Yes, I am,
For there are words out there
That can heal,
And I want to know them . . .
All of them!

There are words of peace,
And I want to play with them
In the playgrounds
Of our humanity . . .
With you

There are words of love
Which are exponential
In all senses of their expression
And waiting to be embraced and to
Embrace as well,
Those who are in need,
Those who are not
And those of us
Who know not the difference . . .
Or are indifferent

Oh, let us not forget
The words of joy!
Won't you put on your smile
And come dance with me . . .
This day?
For who knows,
This day may be
Our last opportunity
To listen

NOW

My ancestors are still waiting
As are many peoples,
Cultures
And ethnicities
Across the fabric
Of humanity

It is time to darn
This worn ragged cloth
Of our existence
And experiential-ness
And make it new again

Time . . .
It is time.
Not tomorrow,
For the time is . . .
NOW!

A change is gonna come ~ Sam Cooke

She

She came from a land
Named "Necessary"
She did not know how
To restrain her voice
Nor that which was
Pushing up and out
From the core of her
Soul

She had a spirit of
Authenticity about her,
And her truth radiated
And joined in the light
Of the world

Wherever she visited,
She left footprints
Of integrity
In the gardens
She left behind

Yes, she was
A wonder to behold
That blinded whomever
By her mere sheer
Grace

Remembering Mommy
Dedicated to all the children of the world

Mommy was a woman of faith,
Strong faith.
After all,
She believed in me . . .
Even when I did not believe in my self.

Whenever I was going
Through something,
It was she whom I sought,
When my heart got
Caught up
In the tangled webs
Of my life,
For which I was
Mostly responsible for.

It was not necessarily her counsel,
But her heart,
Her warm heart,
That of a Mother,
My Mother.

She would always give me
A big hug
And hold me softly,
Securely,
Safely
In her arms
As I laid my head upon her
Bosom,
Just like I did
When I was a small child.

She would rub my head

In a way
That told me she knew

That I was in
A tribulative state.

That woman could look
Into my eyes
And see my soul.
Then, she would
Kiss me upon my forehead.

I remember her words,
Which she borrowed from Psalm 30.
She would whisper into my spirit:
"Joy cometh in the morning"

Momma lived a long life
With long arduous days
And long trying nights,
And has since
Crossed over the horizon
Beyond her final
Sunset.

Me, I am still filled
With the hope
She instilled in my being
As I keep looking
For that overwhelming "Joy"
She spoke of.

I, myself
Have witnessed many
A sunrise,
Many a morning,
Many a night

With beautiful sunsets,
But none of these experiences
Could ever give me that joy,
Peace,
Love

And solace
That I felt
When I laid my head
Upon my Momma's breast,
Listening to her heartbeat.

I remember you, Mommy.
I can still hear
And feel your heartbeat
In me.

I hope you and Daddy are fine.
Please say hello to everyone for me.

The Maori

We know of the oceans
And how they speak
A language,
Calling for us
To venture its waves
And currents.

We look to horizons
And the distant lands,
Waiting to be discovered.

We know of the civil tones
That give cause
For the embrace
Of man
And his humanity.

We know of love,
That of our people
And those we have yet
To meet.

We have an identity
That belongs to
Us alone.

We mark our flesh
With our pride
And ink
As we dance,
Worshipping the Gods
Of Creation.

We are Maori.

Past Times

Old men dreams,
Embraced in the fading
Luminescence
Of the waning moon

Some buried
In the soils
Of the forgotten
Upon the shores
Of lands once visited

Flashing memories
Of the vigor and valor,
Giving cause
For false bravado

The twinkle in their eyes
Long since dulled,
No longer erect
Is their verve,
But their
Semi-virile
And absent-minded ego
Could never admit
Such a thing

Cannot move fast
These days,
Nor do we think
As sharply
As we once prided ourselves,
But I am wise . . .
I think

Life has a way of humbling one
In ways never before considered
In times past

This could never be
An admission
Because every reflection
In every type of mirror
Pictured me
As Superman . . .
Or Jesus Christ

Never considered the weight
Of blasphemy
In my younger days
Because then
I could outrun Karma,
But now that my pace
Has slowed,
She comes bearing gifts . . .
Some heavy weights,
But mostly sweet fruits . . .
So, I must have accidentally
Or unconsciously
Done a few things right

I am still an explorer,
Discovering new pains,
Aches
And a lack of mobility,
But that is okay,
For I still have my dreams
Of a past
I think
Used to be

Of All Things

The minarets towering
In the sky
Betwixt
Heaven and Earth
Above the villages,
The towns,
The country sides . . .

Bearing witness to and of
The people
Who look to them
With hearts of heavy,
Hearts of life

We hear your calls.
Do you hear ours?

Life moves forward
With anticipation
Or neglect,
Yet
At the stated times,
The voice spreads across the land
In a call for prayer

Did the suffering cease?
Was the anguish eased?
Will peace come
In some way
Or another
To all
Who are troubled?

Give me your weak,
Give me your tired,

Give me your poor,
Was another call I heard.
The absurd-ness
Of it all
Is that this was the beginning
Of the end
Of a lie
That was spoken
Much to much

But the minarets
Speak of different things
In a different language,
One that is not
So easily diffused
By the ears of men

Five times a day,
They call to the soul
To fold
Itself
In the arms
Of their Creator
And submit
For a few moments
To that which
Is above all things,
And IS all things . . .

Of all things

As Zion Comes Home . . . to Me!

From the 3rd to the 5th,
Our oddity becomes us
As we prepare to shift across
The place where boundaries
Once existed

The consistence of the fabric
Is failing,
Falling at our feet
That we may tread
And leave invisible footprints
Upon our past

A new consciousness is being birthed
Within old minds,
And we are babes
Once again

There is a twinkle
Within the eye of our soul,
Seeking to behold
Its own reflective truth

Glory Be!

The glass has been cleaned
The hull has been gleaned
The weak are being weaned
And the crippled teats
Of false solace
Are drying up,
For we were never ever nourished
By the lies

And we, the children prayed:
"Now I lay me down to sleep . . ."

But it never came
Until the dawn
When we were called
To turn our chatter off,
To close the portals to our awareness
That they could not poison
The divine seed,
Held in hidden hugs
Within our inner sacredness

And now, the procession begins

The clowns have painted their faces
With exaggerated smiles
And cloaked themselves
In oversized pantaloons
Of pastels and silks

It is time to march
In the piper's parade

The cymbals are crashing
And the crowds are jeering,
Cheering on the brave amongst us,
Hoping they will sacrifice their fears
And thus validate
Their over-inflated false esteems

Are we there yet?

The bets are being placed
On a Cosmic Roulette Wheel,
And we are rushing
To load the guns

Wanna play?

I got one in the chamber

Eclectic Verse

Just for you
It has my name on it,
Etched faintly in sur-reality

This is my gift
Because i love you

Will you hurry and pull the trigger please?

Down on my bleeding knees,
I am still praying for God
To quicken me,
Quicken his pace
And come and tell us the combination
To the lock to Eden's gate
Before we die

I do not wish to perform the task anymore
Of having to bury our brethren
The Christed One did say:
"Let the dead bury the dead."
Well . . . I am tired of digging holes

I am sweating rivulets of melancholy
A strange blood drips
Profusely from my brow
It blinds me

Like a Taurean wanting to charge,
I am seeing red,
But there is no anger for me to embrace,
Not for the Tailor
Nor the Weaver of this cloth of existence

My slothful ways are fading
As if they never were,
And I must gather a new reason
To possibly justify

william s. peters, sr.

My spiritual procrastinations,
And I know I cannot,
For i have smiled in the face
Of my delusions
Once too often

Tell me a story,
Sing me a lullaby, Mommy
That I may slumber . . .

This is the wantonness of the anxious,
But she is at rest
And wishes not to be disturbed
So, ssshhhhhhhhhhhh!
Lest you invoke her wrath
She then will quell
Your Harp-ing

The doves are circling like vultures,
Seeking but a solitary Olive Branch
That they may return
To the place of pairing
Where all wait permission
To exit the Ark

Has your Twin Flame spoken?

Has it stopped raining yet?

I, the Lion begin to hunger,
But they told me
To not bite the hand that feeds me,
But I am carnivorous
And I have a taste
For blood and uncooked meat

Feed me your body,
You self-declared Christ

Eclectic Verse

That I may be sanctified
By the false doctrines you have fed
The other inhabitants
Who voluntarily attended this carnival

You are but a man
As am I

And as we both cling to the myths
Of our belief systems,
Created for man
By man,
We step across the path of righteousness,
Killing in the name of some God
Whom we have never met,
But yet,
Carried within our breast
All of our misunderstood lives

They incessantly ask me:
"What's in your wallet"?

Does it really matter?

In the meantime,
There is an awakening taking place
The coded strands of the ancient "Lore"
Of our construct
Are beginning to resonate
Within the memories of us
Which are paying attention

We were told, we were mere mortals

How can that be,
When He / She / It
Which was perfect and beyond
Made me?

The only light that has failed me
Is the one you gave me control of,
And I have yet to flip the switch
I know it does exist
Somewhere in this abyss
Of my exponential-ness

So, I stand here with but my intentions
Not to mention
My power,
And I refuse to cower anymore,
For . . .
Be it death
Or transition,
It is all the same

And the crippled and
The lame
Shall walk again
And claim their thrones
As we, the drones
Take responsibility
For our own possible demise

My eyes are open now
And I smile within
In a "knowing",
A certainty
As Zion comes home . . . to me

Same

Same origin . . . womb
Same planet . . . Earth
Same heavens . . . look up
Same breath . . . breathe
Same heartbeat . . . listen
Same Sun . . . bathe
Same stars . . . wonder

Perniciousness

The ignorance prevails
As the rhetoric assails
The expressions
Of those who think not
For themselves

The culling of the herd
Serves the few
Who know
And always knew
The truth

Be it
Apartheid,
Racism
Or Genocide,
They lied
And told us
What they need us
To go along with,
Act on
Now and then
And once upon . . .
All the time

Shine On!

I am but a child
Conceived,
Nurtured,
Spawned
From the light, infused,
Amniotic fluid
In the womb
Of the universe . . .
As were you

My own light
Is enshrouded
In a darkness
That abides about abundantly
Around everything brilliant

It is not the color
Of my skin,
My religiosity,
My politics,
Nor anything else
That these
Surreptitious, sneaky shadows seek
To quiet
Or extinguish,
But the inevitable coming
Of my knowing
Of the power I
One light possesses

I am a city,
Climbing this hill
I call light,
And some day again
I shall rest upon

The foundations of that rock
That is called a mountain,
And all shall see
Just as The Christed One
Spoke of
In the beauty
Of the Beatitudes

The lowly
Shall be exalted,
The reverent
Shall be praised,
The compassionate
Shall be embraced,
The truthful
Shall come to know of themselves

I no longer fear those
Who come wielding bushels
To cover my candle,
For my flame
Is everlasting
As is thine own

I now am rending the curtains
That would cloak my divinity,
For it is ordained . . .
That is what we light-souls
Have come to do,
That alone is our charge . . .
To shine on

In spite of the trials,
The tribulations . . .
Shine on!

Of Dreams . . .

Dancing upon the waves
Of thoughtful expressions
Yet to come . . .
Though the seas are tumultuous,
I dance anyway

I saw my hidden dreams
Peek between my thoughts,
Beckoning me to take a chance
And follow the path they were foraging
Through my wilderness

There was a canopy of fear
That embraced the path before me,
And doubt added sharp pebbles
That they may trouble
My bared feet

The lore was enticing enough . . .
So, I summoned a bit of courage
And began to go forth

Every step offered
Some kind of a painful reminder
Of the deluded comfort
I willingly
Left behind

Was it solace
Or ignorance?

There was a light
Ahead of me, but in my ways,
I doubted its validity
And wanted so much

To claim it as illusion
What have I allowed my self
To become
In those days
Of no fortitude
To challenge life?

I began to reflect upon my past . . .
Sure, I have experienced
And accomplished many things,
But I never did smell the potential
Of what I could, become . . . did I?

No, I will not be minimized
Nor marginalized by my own doing!
Never again, I say to my self,
But I know that is another lie
I tell my self . . .

So, I close my eyes
As I dance upon
The waves of what may be
As I navigate my way down
The path of Dreams

I dance anyway

The End Game

It matters not how you got there,
For in the end,
We become captives
Of the place we inhabit.

We can reflect
All we wish to,
But it does not alter
The journey
One iota.

Yes, there are lessons
For those
Who wish to learn
And those who wish to
Teach,
But which truth
Is certifiably
Without question
For all?

We have been shrouded
By darkness
Since the beginning
Of time.
Darkness has always
Surrounded the light . . .

Keep your candle lit,
My friend,
For the end game
Awaits to consume
The errant wanderer

Who aimlessly,
Mindlessly
Walks,
Meanders,
Through life.

Hate begets hate.
Love begets love.

Hate and Love are energies.
Be mindful of which you feed!

The End Game

Today and Every Day

The flowers are wilting.
The fragrance of humanity
Is somewhat becoming pungent
As we continue to allow.

I shall plant new seeds of light
   Of love
      Wherever I go
That we may harvest once again
Our joy,
   Our gratitude,
      Our compassion.

This is what I choose to nurture . . . humanity.

                This is my charge.

Today and every day.

                What is yours?

Eclectic Verse

I have laughed my way
Through a
River of tears,
Rebuking the strains
That challenged my
Unsoiled delusional
Reality

i looked skewed
Through the narrow slits
And cracked lens
Of my awareness,
And the bewitching hour
Screamed malcontent

Let us walk the plank,
Me, myself & i
And cast ourselves
Into the ocean
That we may drown
The whispers
That wish us no peace

Eclectic Verse

Am i unified...
As one,
Balanced and focused,
Or but a collection
Of singularities,
Masquerading,
Pretending, i can read
The script?

i so like dancing
To the symphonious discord
Life presents,
And at times,
i attempt to sing along,
But i do not know the words,
So, i guess my way
Through the wilderness,
Looking for a path
Of validation

i leave some thoughts behind me
Like Hansel and Gretel,
Should i need to retrace my steps...

william s. peters, sr.

But my abiding fear is
That i am alone . . . now
As i have always been,
And all i truly have
To accompany me
Are the whispers
Of eclectic verse . . .

Mommy, can you hear them?

Eclectic Verse

Epilogue

about William S. Peters, Sr.

AKA 'just bill', William S. Peters, Sr. is a devoted writer who has been committed to the path of poetry since 1966. Presently, his poetic work has been published in excess of 200 anthologies, newspapers and literary magazines, including about 50 books of his own. Since the day of his commitment to the creation and public-sharing of the poetic art, Peters has been a devoted supporter of the venue of creative expression –regardless of form. His conviction that the human countenance through written art is a necessity reflects in his capacity as an activist for the progression and evolution of humanity and its love of each other.

The author has been able to publish many first-time writers and poets from across the globe through hands-on assistance, counseling and guidance; thus, introducing their work of different literary genres to the public. In its brief history, Inner Child Press International – Peters' publishing enterprise has brought attention worldwide to thousands of poets by means of the authors' personal releases and the appearances of their work in a large number of anthologies. Such undertakings encompass notable and highly acclaimed anthology series, such as the voluminous *World Healing, World Peace* – published every two years since 2012 and *The Year of the Poet* – a monthly international book as conceived in January 2014 and published every month since. In the latter anthology, The Poetry Posse –a core group of contributing poets comprises between fourteen and eighteen poets from a large variety of world regions. This publication also features between two and four guest poets each month.

William S. Peters, Sr. possesses one other passion: To induct less commonly represented cultures into the mainstream entity of the "West". To materialize this predilection, he has – among other globally collaborative works, published *Voices from Iraq*, *Kurdish Voices*, *Aleppo, Palestine* and the encyclopedic *Balkan Anthology* while he, all along has been – to adopt his words – 'building bridges of cultural understanding'.

In September 2015, the author was recognized as the "Poet Laureate" at the Kosovo International Poetry Festival in Rahovec. His sizeable book, *The Vine Keeper* was showcased there where he was also awarded The Golden Grape Award for it. Being so inspired by this communion of poets, Peters went on to pen his book of tribute, *O Sweet Kosovo . . . Dreams of Rahovec*. This work has been since translated into Albanian by Fahredin Shehu, the esteemed poet and scholar who has incorporated it into the Rahovec School System in 2017.

From the 2015 inaugural formal introduction into the world of international poetry onward, invitations to William S. Peters, Sr. grew in speed and frequency. In 2016, he attended the Morocco International Poetry Festival in Rabat as an invited participant and Key Note speaker. He made many friends also in that world region, impressing them with his spiritual essence which was serving all efforts pertaining the plight of humanity. In 2017, Peters' journey continued through a dazzling tour to Strumica, Macedonia; Monastir, Tunisia; Casablanca and Larache, Morocco; Istanbul, Turkey; Rome, Italy; Amman, Jordan; Bethlehem, Mar Saba, Ramallah and West Bank, Palestine, and Chicago, USA.

The author has been immensely inspired in his travels and has penned a large number of poems and prose pieces during and after his introduction to the places of his personal experiencing. Several of those poetry collections have been included in *Tunisia, My Love* and *7 Days in Palestine . . . the Land, the People, the Blood, the Tears and the Laughter*. Peters was commissioned to write the book on Tunisia which was launched in 2018 at the Poetry by the Sea Festival in Monastir, Tunisia. He is presently working on an extensive book, *The Journey . . . Footprints and Shadows*, which will chronicle via poetry his complete touring between September 2nd and November 9th 2017.

William S. Peters, Sr., a 2016 Pulitzer Prize nominee for poetry has enjoyed the honor of being recognized for his work at large – publishing and writing alike also in the U.S., his country of birth. The number of his appearances on North American radio and television shows is too copious to list. His poetic work has been published in various countries of the world, including Kosovo, Albania, Germany, Iran, Iraq, India, The Philippines, Taiwan, Canada, Italy, Romania, Saudi Arabia, Jordan, Morocco, Italy, England, Romania, France, and Poland. The author is known to be adamant about taking time out to share his humanitarian, spiritual and philosophical insights wherever he is invited. He has cited and performed his poetry at numerous venues, such as summer camps for children, teacher workshops, poetry workshops and classrooms, including an October 2017-lecture to graduate students at The University of Jordan in Amman, Jordan.

The author currently serves as the CEO of Inner Child Enterprises, ltd., Managing Director of Inner Child Press International, Executive Producer of Inner Child Radio and Executive Editor of Inner Child Magazine. He says: "I have always likened Life to that of a Garden. So, for me, Life is simply about the Seeds We Sow and Nourish. All things we 'Think and Do', will 'Be' Cause and eventually manifest themselves in an 'Effect' within our own personal 'Existences' and 'Experiences' . . . whether it be Fruit, Flowers, Weeds or Barren Landscapes!" In high regard of the "Fruits of his Labor", William S. Peters, Sr. wishes that everyone would thus go on to plant "Lovely Seeds" on "Good Ground" in their own "Gardens of Life".

For more of William S. Peters, Sr., visit his personal web site at:
www.iamjustbill.com

a few words from Fahredin B. Shehu

Despite the fact that I have known the poetry of William S. Peters for over half a decade, the poet / man does not cease to amaze me; for, he is an embodiment of human goodness, values, ingenuity and much more. This work by the author is not the first that I had the privilege to write about. Still, every new reading opportunity offers me a unique experience of his "Word" in the true sense of the term. For a poet like myself, a word is at times a curse; at other times, a blessing, and sometimes . . . both at once, intertwined in an ethereal thread of a spool of creativity.

Throughout my extensive journey in aesthetics, I happened to realize four levels of creativity: skill, art, theurgy and revelation. In this masterful work, Peters demonstrates all three of the aforementioned, with 'skill' functioning like the top note of a symphonic composition or the summit of a pyramidal layering of the artistic quest, as reflected through poetry. As if to shed light on this phenomenon, he eloquently utters: "Not every poem needs to be about flowers and butterflies. This poem was written about Love and the lack thereof." Throughout *Eclectic Verse*, the reader will find the author transcend his entire content material into a fluid expression of whims and wishes, quests and questions, longings and belongings, understandings and misunderstandings, affirmations and confirmations, illumination and omnipresence of the Plethora of Mankind, and Creation's vibrations that oscillate in time and space, which we perceive as reality.

William S. Peters, Sr. delivers poetry that is so simple, so flowing, yet so intense that he lends life to the gyrations of the Soul – since as, per poetry, nothing is too far; as for soul, nothing is unattainable; as for spirit, there is no distance or blindness, and finally, as for brain, there is only a dawn of thoughts that illuminates the entire being. In his poem, "Critique", the author confirms this assertion: "Yes, Black is beautiful, / But many see it as a threat, / A blight on humanity, / A nuisance / That disturbs their / False solace. / BTW, you are beautiful too, / Regardless of your hued-ness / Or the lack thereof."

In *Eclectic Verse*, Peters gives readers another challenge to encounter on their poetic journey, one that comes as an invite to engage in his creative use of form. He successfully transforms his readership into active participants of his experience of poetry's external offerings. With the following poem, in particular, the author demonstrates once again that Poetry is limitless.

meop sdrawkcab eht

deredro eb tsum ti taht smees efil
dnatsrednu nac ew taht
sredrob eht txiwteb stsixe efil taht
dnamed yb dehsilbatse

epacse ot gniyrt ma i tub
etor dna etir lla morf
os robal od i yhw si hcihw
eton elpmis siht etirw ot

What an incredible, soothing, thrilling, challenging and highly artistic book!

Fahredin Shehu
January, 2019
Kosovo

Poet, Philosopher, Essayist
Director and Organizer, International Poetry Festival in Kosovo (1st in 2015)
Author of *Nun, Invisible Plurality, Nektarina, Elemental 99, Kun, Dismantle of Hate, Crystalline Echoes, Pleroma's Dew, Emerald Macadam, Maelstrom, Neon Child* and HERENOW

A Selection of the Author's Other Books

available at . . .

www.innerchildpress.com

www.iamjustbill.com

and other fine bookstores

7 Days in Palestine

william s. peters sr.

O Sweet Kosovo

... dreams of Rahovec

Poetry & Prose

by

William S. Peters, Sr.

Inward Reflections

Think on These Things
Book II

william s. peters, sr.

Morocco Love

المغرب يا حُبّي

william s. peters, sr.

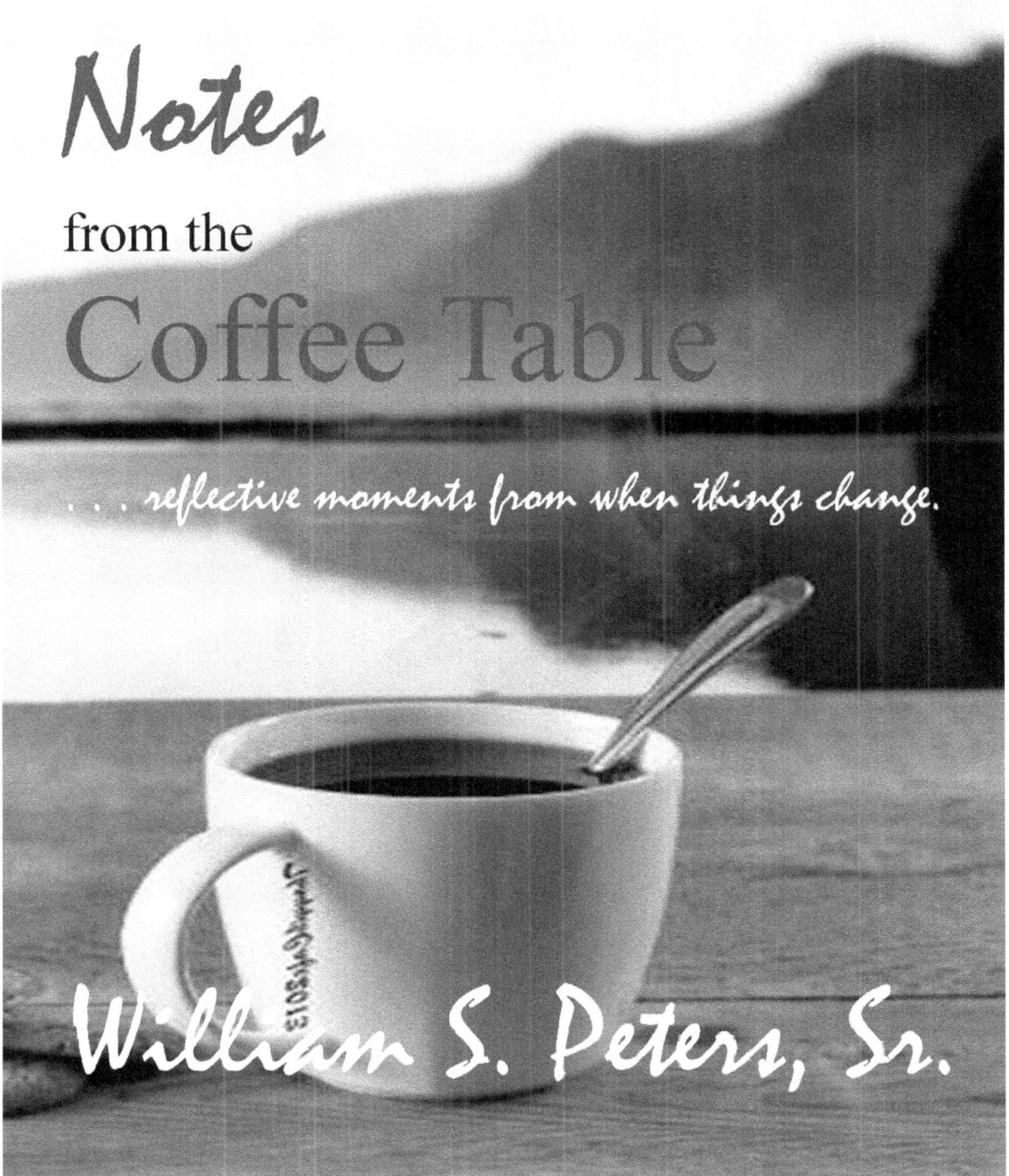

Confucius say...

william s. peters, sr.

inner child press
presents

Tunisia My Love

william s. peters, sr.

it's all about the Love ... baby !

william s. peters, sr.

Day by Day

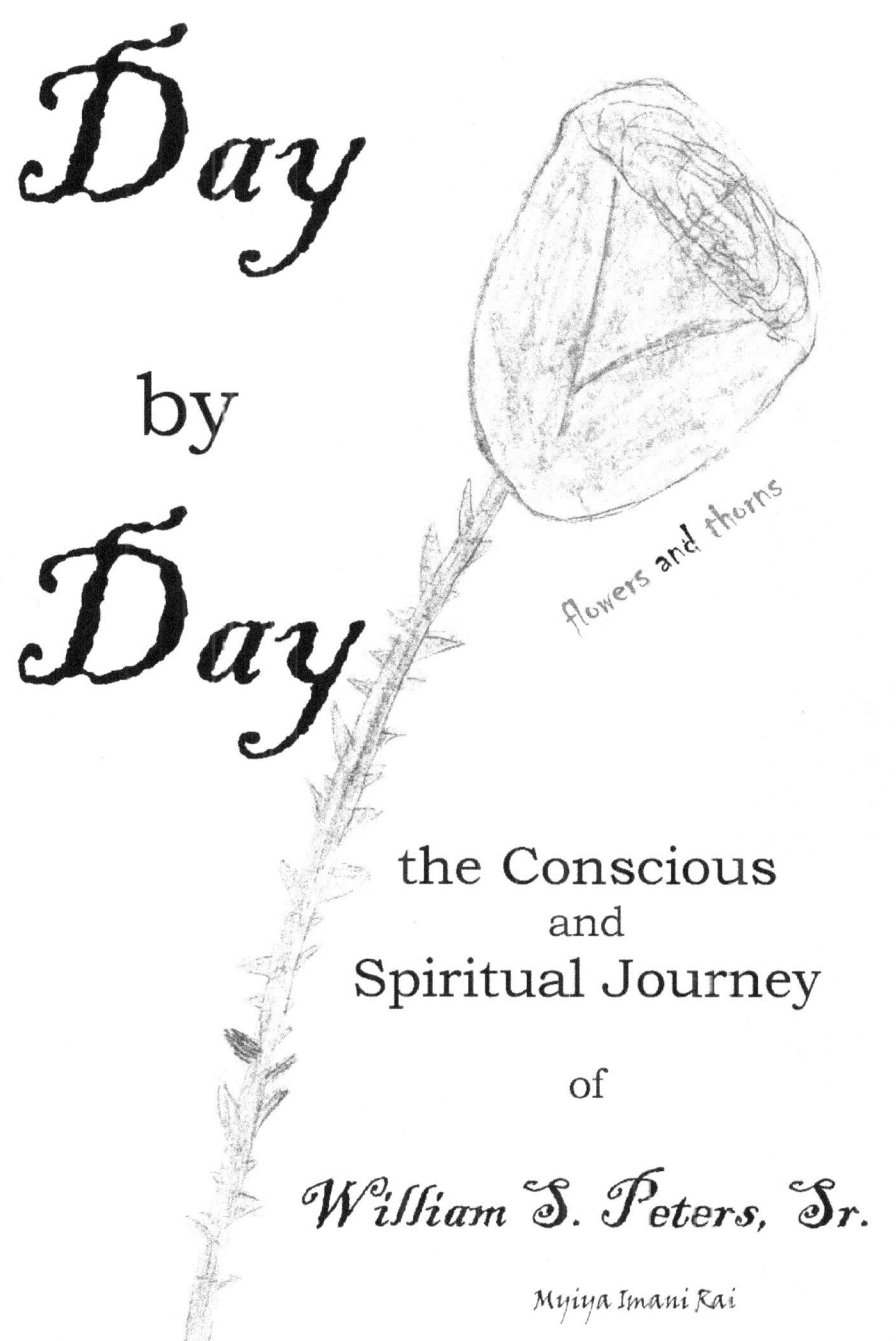

flowers and thorns

the Conscious
and
Spiritual Journey

of

William S. Peters, Sr.

Myiya Imani Rai

my inner garden

~ expressions and discoveries ~
by
William S. Peters, Sr.

Inner Child Press

Inner Child Press is a publishing company founded and operated by writers. Our personal publishing experiences provide us an intimate understanding of the sometimes-daunting challenges writers, new and seasoned may face in the business of publishing and marketing their creative "Written Work".

For more information

Inner Child Press

www.innerchildpress.com

intouch@innerchildpress.com

Inner Child Press International

'building bridges of cultural understanding'

202 Wiltree Court, State College, Pennsylvania 16801

www.ingramcontent.com/pod-product-compliance
Lightning Source LLC
Chambersburg PA
CBHW081831170426
43199CB00017B/2701